PREACHiNG POiNTS

PREACHiNG POiNTS

55 Tips for Improving Your Pulpit Ministry

Edited by Scott M. Gibson

Contributions by
Haddon W. Robinson
Jeffrey D. Arthurs
Patricia M. Batten
Scott M. Gibson
Matthew D. Kim

LEXHAM PRESS

Preaching Points: 55 Tips for Improving Your Pulpit Ministry
© 2016 by Scott M. Gibson

Lexham Press, 1313 Commercial St., Bellingham, WA 98225
LexhamPress.com

First edition by Weaver Book Company.

Print ISBN 9781683592082
Digital ISBN 9781683592099

Cover: Frank Gutbrod
Interior design and typesetting: { In a Word }
Editing: Line for Line Publishing Services

To our former, present, and future students—that they preach faithfully God's Word.

Contents

Acknowledgments

Words of thanks may seem cheap or paltry when it comes to the herculean effort that others play in the production of any project, not the least of which this book. But the expression of gratitude is one that demonstrates one's indebtedness to others—for the publication of this book is one of dependence upon others.

First, thank you, Haddon Robinson, Jeffrey Arthurs, Matthew Kim, and Patricia Batten for your role with the production of Preaching Points, the podcast. Your commitment to preaching is impressive.

Second, a hearty thanks to those who have helped in the production of Preaching Points, the podcast. The coordinators of the Haddon W. Robinson Center for Preaching—past and present—have all had a hand in recording and editing the podcasts. These incredible partners include Jairus Hallums, Paul Gard, Peter Frey, Chris Rappazini, and Eric Dokken. Thank you so very, very much! With great appreciation I thank Brian Hettinga, whose final production engineering has made the weekly podcasts sparkle. You're the best, Brian!

Third, is an expression of appreciation to Tim Norton for his incredible assistance in moving this book forward. Thank you, Tim, my boy. In addition, thanks to David Giese for his transcription work for Jeff Arthurs and thanks to Josh Cahan for his transcription work for Matt Kim. Your help has been immeasurable.

Fourth, thanks to Gordon-Conwell's graphic designer Nicole Rim for her concept of the Preaching Points logo, which now is incorporated into the cover for this book. Her artistic contributions to the seminary and to the Center for Preaching are certainly not unnoticed. Thank you, Nicole!

Fifth, thanks to Jim Weaver and Weaver Book Company. Your amazing commitment to preaching has advanced the cause of preaching and is helping preachers all over the world. Thank you, thank you, thank you!

Finally, thank you to my wife, Rhonda, who never ceases to amaze me with her support and love. She understands the importance of a clear idea—hers is an unrelenting commitment to Christ in all areas of life and she reminds me of that idea every day in how she lives and loves.

The Authors

Scott M. Gibson (D.Phil., Oxford) is the Haddon W. Robinson Professor of Preaching and Ministry and director of the Center for Preaching at Gordon-Conwell Theological Seminary and co-founder of the Evangelical Homiletics Society.

Haddon W. Robinson (Ph.D., Southern Illinois University) is the Harold John Ockenga Distinguished Professor of Preaching Emeritus at Gordon-Conwell Theological Seminary, South Hamilton, MA.

Jeffrey D. Arthurs (Ph.D., Purdue University) is Professor of Preaching and Communication at Gordon-Conwell Theological Seminary, South Hamilton, MA.

Matthew D. Kim (Ph.D., University of Edinburgh) is Assistant Professor of Preaching and Ministry at Gordon-Conwell Theological Seminary, South Hamilton, MA.

Patricia M. Batten (D.Min., Gordon-Conwell Theological Seminary) is Ranked Adjunct Assistant Professor of Preaching at Gordon-Conwell Theological Seminary, South Hamilton, MA.

Introduction

This book is about communicating ideas. When we read, speak, write, or preach we are conveying ideas. The preacher has the responsibility to be clear to his or her listeners. If there were to be an eleventh commandment given to preachers it probably would be "Be clear!"

We want preachers to be clear—and we want to be clear. We want to communicate the idea of the passage on which we're preaching. We want our listeners to comprehend the idea and connect with it, applying it to their lives.

Preaching Points is a collection of some of the best of the hundreds of Preaching Points that the Haddon W. Robinson Center for Preaching at Gordon-Conwell Theological Seminary has produced. Preaching Points is a weekly podcast on iTunes U that features conversations on preaching by Haddon Robinson, Jeffrey Arthurs, Matthew Kim, and Patricia Batten—all members of the preaching faculty of Gordon-Conwell Theological Seminary, South Hamilton campus.

In brief reflections on preaching we put into practice the commandment for clarity as we address one idea about preaching and drive it home for our listeners—and now our readers.

Podcast listeners have asked for a printed version of Preaching Points. This book is an answer to their request and, hopefully, an avenue to connect with even more preachers to help them to commit themselves to preaching the idea of the text and be clear in how they do it.

Readers will note that the Preaching Points topics vary as they relate to preaching: the preacher's spiritual life, the way we preach, the way we live life as preachers, our role as a preacher, considerations for listeners—and much more.

In addition, readers are treated to a variety of authors indicated by their initials at the beginning of each Preaching Point: Haddon Robinson (HWR), Jeffrey Arthurs (JDA), Matthew Kim (MDK), Patricia Batten (PMB), and myself (SMG), all experienced preachers and teachers of preaching.

I trust you'll benefit from what you read—and that what you learn from the Preaching Points you'll put into practice in your life and in your preaching.

SCOTT M. GIBSON, EDITOR

Preach the Big Idea I

HWR

We talk about the Big Idea at Gordon-Conwell Theological Seminary. The Big Idea is the dominant idea in your sermon. It's made up by asking two questions: First, what is the author talking about? And second, what is the author saying about what he is talking about?

We try to crystalize it into an idea that addressees people in the twenty-first century. It is important to realize that, in the sermon, this idea—the Big Idea—is what has to come through. Sermons have all sorts of ideas. If you think about it in terms of an outline, you have Roman numerals—they're all ideas. Under the Roman numerals, you have A, B, and C—they're all ideas. Maybe under A, you have 1 and 2—they're ideas. All of these ideas come together to get the sermon's *central idea* across to your listeners.

Put it this way: The Big Idea of good preaching is Preach the Big Idea. I'm not talking about minimizing what you do in your sermon. I'm saying that the introduction begins to lead to that idea, the supporting material (i.e., Roman numerals) support that idea, and the conclusion drives home that idea.

People learn by ideas. Very few people will ever be able to duplicate your outline a week after you give the sermon. In fact, if you ask your spouse or friend what you preached about a week ago, you may find that it puts a strain on your relationship.

But, if you can take that idea and drive it home—show people where it comes from in the Bible, how this relates to where they live today, illustrate it, apply it, and make the Big Idea the big idea of your sermon—you'll find that it is more effective.

People can't handle a whole bunch of ideas that seem unrelated. You will give them something to live by, something to die by, if they have ideas that control their lives. The Bible is a book of ideas. It has poetry, narrative, parables, literature, etc., but it is basically a book of ideas. All of these different genres are getting at an idea. As you preach, you ought to know what that idea is in the text and what it is for your people. Then drive it home—nail it into their minds and into their lives. The Big Idea of good preaching is Preach the Big Idea. I hope you're doing that and I hope you'll keep on doing that.

Go to the Bible to hear God speak

PMB

I have the privilege of teaching beginning students how to preach. One of their first assignments is to select a passage. I always ask students, "How do you know which passage to preach?" In a parish pulpit ministry context, the answers are (1) the amount of time I have to preach might determine my passage or (2) the needs of the congregation. We talk about the importance of a preaching calendar. I'm not sure how my students choose a passage. When I've asked, one response stands out: "This passage really preaches."

There's a difference between studying a text because of its pulpit potential or preachability versus studying a text to hear God speak.

I've heard Haddon Robinson warn scores of students not to go to the Bible looking for a sermon.

How do you approach the Bible when you prepare to preach?

Preaching is an enormous task and it comes around every week. Ready or not, here it comes! You have other ministry responsibilities that are bearing down on you. You can see why a preacher might just want to get the thing written and be done with it. And, the Bible is, after all, the preacher's main tool.

But it's also the Word of God. And responsible preachers

remember that the Bible is God's Word. It's a revelation of Him. We go to the Bible to hear a word from God.

We too often approach the Bible with a "what can this passage do for me" kind of outlook. Will this passage make me look interesting, knowledgeable, creative? Like squeezing the juice from a lemon, all we want to do is squeeze a sermon out of the passage.

But when we do that, it's a recipe for a sour sermon. We've lost something very important. It's the belief that the Bible is the Word of God. It's the understanding that when the Bible speaks, God speaks.

When you prepare to preach this week, don't go to a passage looking for a sermon. Go to the Bible to hear God speak. And when you hear God speak, then you can preach—really preach. Go to the Bible to hear God speak.

Soak yourself in the text 3

MDK

Charles Spurgeon once encouraged preachers by saying, "Soak yourself in the text." What is he talking about? Is he talking about giving ourselves a homiletical bath? Yes, in many ways, he is. He's asking us to meditate, to ponder, and to immerse ourselves in the Word of God. The image is one of being submersed in water, to be covered by the Word of God—that we allow God's Word to cleanse us, to purify us, and to give us a renewed sense of excitement. The Word of God washes over our dirty bodies and cleanses us in such a way that we are able to see His Word in a new light.

Preaching is difficult. We're attempting to take the historical context of when the Bible was written and "bridge the gap," as the late John Stott said, to bring God's Word into the contemporary world. And this isn't easy.

For many of us, if we're honest about our sermon preparation, sometimes we focus so much on today, and the world of today, that we lose sight of what was going on back when the biblical author was writing. But when we soak ourselves in the text, we're allowing God's Word to come at us from different angles. It's a multi-perspectival approach to reading the Word. Different genres and different moods intertwine with how we're reading and interpreting the text.

I have heard that the late John Stott repetitively read the

3

Word for the sermon passage that he was preaching on. Wherever he was, whether he was waiting for the doctor or sitting in a bus waiting for his transportation to take him to where he needed to go, he would pull out his Bible and read that passage over and over and over again. He would meditate on it. He would reflect on it. He would soak deeply in the Word of God.

In our sermon preparation, we're often quick to tackle homiletics rather than engage rigorously in hermeneutics. We're thinking about outlines. We're thinking about delivery. We're thinking about gestures. We're thinking about how we're going to communicate this truth. But such habits reinforce a shallow or cursory reading of the text. Soaking ourselves in the text creates space to slow down. It allows us to meditate and ponder and really "breathe in" all that God has to teach us from that passage. Preaching is as much about communication to others as it is communicating to ourselves. We are also the recipients of God's Word. We allow God's Word to hit us first as Robinson's definition conveys. It's something that we apply to ourselves first. One of the dangers that we can avoid if we're immersing ourselves, if we're really soaking ourselves in the text, is to be able to see how this passage speaks directly into my life.

As we preach this week, take a moment to plan your week out. How much time do you devote to sermon preparation? How much time do you devote to, in particular, exegesis? Do we go through a historical, grammatical, and literary study of the passage in its context? Do we allow those three aspects of sermon preparation to be the foundation on which we build a sermon? Or, perhaps because of the busy rhythm of life, we're constantly thinking about how to communicate these truths without really taking the time to exegete the passage and apply it to ourselves. I want to encourage you to slow down. And maybe this week, just as Charles Spurgeon encourages us, "Soak yourself in the text."

Being biblical and contemporary is the art of Christian communication

HWR

Some time ago I went to church—I go to church regularly—and on this particular Sunday I did not have any responsibilities (i.e., I didn't have to preach, I didn't have to read the Scriptures). I had some friends who went with me. They were folks who, if you were taking a religious survey, would check "churchgoer occasionally." One of these friends said that, when he and his wife go to church, they don't like the music. They're always singing the same old thing: "O Little Town of Bethlehem" or "Up from the Grave He Arose." These were not regular attenders, but they went that Sunday with me. Our pastor wasn't there. A guest preacher—a professor at one of our Christian colleges—was to preach and he had obviously done his homework. He was preaching on 1 Peter 1 and he had done his work in the Greek. He took us through it and told us how important it was. When the sermon was over and we were going home, the folks wanted to be polite. They gave the kind of compliments that, for any pastor, are an insult. "I like the way he dressed. . . . He really is an intelligent, educated man." What happened was the sermon was all in 1 Peter. It was about the long-ago and far-away and it never made it into the twenty-first century.

Good sermons are nailed to the text. They are biblical. If we don't preach the Bible, we have nothing to preach. If you want to preach politics, there are better people out there who can preach politics. If you want to preach psychology, there are better psychologists on television. But we can preach the Bible. The danger of preaching the Bible (if there is a danger) is that it's all about the long-ago and far-away. So people hear sermons and they leave sitting in judgment on Abraham for going down to Egypt or upset with Jonah because he ran away from God and we never get to where the people in the pew are.

Good sermons live with that tension. They live with the tension of the Bible and they also live with the tension of being relevant to the folks who are listening. I've sometimes said that we don't teach the Bible; we teach *people* the Bible. The task of preaching is not just to help people understand the biblical texts, as important as that is; it is to help people understand how the biblical text relates to them. Quite frankly, both of these deserve our attention.

I find that expository preachers often do not really ask, What's the purpose of this sermon? What should it do in people's lives? If you say, "Why are you preaching on Romans 5?" some preachers answer, "Well, because last week I was in Romans 4. Next week I'll be in Romans 6." Until we have figured out why the passage would be important to people today—not just tell them that but show them that (e.g., How would it work in their business? How would it work in their homes? How does it work in their thinking?) as we bring the biblical text and the modern world together—we haven't done our job. So we are not preaching to people about the Bible. We are preaching to people *about them* from the Bible. And that means that there are two tensions: the tension of the biblical text (crucial, vital, and important) and the tension of the folks who are listening to us. Good preachers work hard to see to it that their sermons have that balance of biblical truth and contemporary relevance. That's why being biblical and contemporary is the art of Christian communication.

Speaking truth to people takes moral courage

HWR

I've been teaching preaching now for almost fifty years. That's a long time. Over the years, I have seen a lot of changes, but it seems to me that one of the things that is desperately needed in those who lead Christian congregations today is moral courage. I'm not talking about just ordinary courage such as the kind of courage it takes to play football and risk being knocked down; or the courage it takes to stand up to somebody in the church that is really trying to put you down. Certainly, I'm not talking about Rambo courage where you knock people down if they disagree with you. I'm talking about *moral* courage: to be able to speak truth with power, to be able to speak truth to people who don't necessarily want to hear it. If you go back to your Old Testament and look at the prophets, it seems to me that many of them had moral courage, courage to speak the truth to people who did not want to hear it or to people who could punish them for speaking it.

Where does moral courage come from? Let me suggest that it comes from realizing who your listeners are. When I was taking graduate work at the University of Illinois, I had a professor who used to say that the thing that marks the professional from the amateur is that if you ask an amateur to speak, the first question is, What will I talk about? while if you ask a professional to speak the first question is, Who is my audience? If you think about it, you and I have an audience of One. Scripture says the Lord speaks through us. It says the Lord gives us His word from the Word. It's when we have that Word to speak that we speak in faithfulness to God. When you realize that you have an audience of One, God Himself, and that ultimately our task is to please Him, to preach so that He is honored, then you have moral courage to say what you might not say in any other way.

We face a society that is antagonistic to many of our values and to our basic message. We have people who are caught up in the push of that society. So, today, to preach well is to preach with moral courage. We can get moral courage if we figure out who our listeners are. We have an audience of One. God is listening, and we need to be sure that what we say pleases Him. Speaking truth to people takes moral courage.

We need scholarly evangelists and evangelistic scholars   6

HWR

It was the year 1704. Two men were born that year. One man was Jonathan Edwards. Jonathan Edwards was a learned pastor in Massachusetts. Yale University has taken his sermons and reprinted them. He is termed as one of the three great intellectuals that the United States has ever produced. He was a man who, in 1741, preached a sermon called "Sinners in the Hands of an Angry God." It was a strange sermon for a man like Jonathan Edwards to preach, but he preached it with passion and the people of his day responded. There was a great movement of God in New England; historians call it the Great Awakening. Jonathan Edwards was a scholar with an evangelist's heart.

The other man who was born in 1704 was John Wesley. John Wesley was an evangelist. The whole Methodist movement came out of his preaching. But he was also a scholar. As he rode on horseback, week after week for thousands of miles, he edited a Greek New Testament. He was an evangelist, but he was also a scholar.

It strikes me that those two men model a great truth: We need scholarly evangelists and evangelistic scholars. Unfortunately, we've had people who are evangelists who seem to have very little to say. They tell story after story with nothing in between—the kind of preaching that is popular but profitless. The good evangelists are people who have taken the Bible seriously, who have studied it and understand it. As pastors and leaders, we need to be sure that we understand the message of the gospel, understand it clearly, and understand the attacks on it when we do evangelism. We need scholarly evangelists.

We also need evangelistic scholars. We need people who take the Bible seriously, who know how to read it, some in the Hebrew and some in the Greek, people who love their books. We need those kinds of people to have a passion and a heart for the lost. You've met some of them in the seminary—folks who can attend great conferences that scholars attend. But, on the other hand, they have a love for Jesus Christ and when they are with non-Christians, they are able to speak to them effectively about the gospel. I have a friend like that, an Old Testament scholar who passes muster in any scholarly group. Again and again I have seen him as he has met people on planes or at Starbucks. He will begin a conversation and, before long, is able to share the gospel. We need that today, don't we?

So, my plea is simply—wherever you are on the spectrum—if you have an evangelist gift, don't give up on study; if you have the ability to do scholarly work, don't give up on evangelism. We need scholarly evangelists and evangelistic scholars.

Sermon preparation is twenty hours of prayer

MDK

It's something that we all know in our minds. We've considered it. But it's often difficult to put into practice. What am I talking about? Pastor R. Kent Hughes, who pastored College Church in Wheaton, IL, for some twenty-seven years, once had this to say about preaching. He said, "Sermon preparation is twenty hours of prayer." Twenty hours? What does he mean? How can we pray for twenty hours when we have so many things to do in ministry?

But what Hughes means is that prayer is extremely valuable in sermon preparation. Prayer is indispensable. We need to pray, because we're engaged in a spiritual battle. The moment we walk up into the pulpit we recognize that what we are doing is not something that just any communicator does. We're preaching God's Word. And the enemy doesn't want us to. The enemy doesn't want us to have power. He doesn't want us to display God's power through our sermon.

What we're doing is bathing our sermon in prayer. How do we do that? It begins when we select a text. I know that there are moments in pastoral ministry where I just thought, *What does the church need to hear?* And so I would just simply go to a text or look for a text. But to have this attitude of sermon preparation being twenty hours of prayer means that from the moment I think about a given sermon, I'm given to prayer. I'm seeking

7

God's guidance. I ask, "God, what do you want me to learn from this particular passage? Which passage should I preach on?" As we're going through the rigors of exegesis and determining what the author is talking about, I'm constantly prayerful. What does it mean to pray in such a way that we're asking the Holy Spirit to guide us to understand the authorial intent of the passage? What does this mean for the people back in Bible times, and what does it mean for us today? Even in outlining or writing our manuscript, we're constantly soaking our sermon in prayer. We're praying through what it means to speak to people in such a way that God's Word comes alive in their midst.

One of the ways we can do this practically speaking is praying through the church directory. Pray about your congregation's needs and struggles. What is that family going through at this moment? What does it look like for this person who has lost her job to understand this particular passage? And as we do so, we slow down our preparation. We don't just rush through it to get the sermon finished. We don't just go through the exercise of exegesis. But we are prayerful about each moment of the sermon preparation process.

A few years ago I was standing on the curb. I remember it vividly. I was a candidate for a pastoral position at a church. One of the pastors on the church staff looked at me. But he didn't just look at me. He gave me one of those up-and-down glances which made me feel uncomfortable. He inquired, "Matt, so how many hours do you pray each day?" I thought to myself, *Hours? I think in minutes.* But what he was really getting at is, "Do you have a deep and profound relationship with the Lord?" D. L. Moody was known to say, "He who kneels the most, stands the best." That's what R. Kent Hughes may have in view when he wisely encourages: Sermon preparation is twenty hours of prayer.

Match the mood of the text

8

MDK

In Philippians 1:3 the Apostle Paul writes, "I thank my God every time I remember you. In all of my prayers for all of you, I always pray with joy." The mood of this text is one of encouragement. It's one of love. It's one of support. And sometimes when we're preaching, the mood of the text may not match the tone of what's written in the Word of God. I want to encourage us to match the mood of the text.

That was an example from Paul's letter to the Philippians. Now hear this one from Psalm 134. It's a song of ascent, a song of praise, a song that was sung as people marched up the hill to be with the Lord and with one another. "Praise the Lord, all you servants of the Lord who minister by night in the house of the Lord. Lift up your hands in the sanctuary and praise the Lord. May the Lord, the Maker of heaven and earth, bless you from Zion." You'll notice the tone. It's one of exultation. It's one of praise. It's one of joy. And we want to have our sermons match the mood of the text.

Let me give you another text from Galatians 1:6–7. It's actually one of stern rebuke, where Paul writes to the church in Galatia, "I am astonished that you are so quickly deserting the one who called you by the grace of Christ and are turning to a different gospel—which is really no gospel at all." We can hear the frustration, perhaps anger—righteous anger that Paul

17

has toward the Galatians as he writes this stern warning that they have deserted the gospel of Jesus Christ.

Sometimes as we're thinking about how we're going to preach a particular passage, we don't necessarily think about the mood of the text. What was Paul feeling as he wrote his letters? What emotions did David experience during his lament to God? What were the Gospel writers going through as they recounted Jesus' life and ministry? What was their mood? What was their attitude? How were they feeling as they wrote to the people? Were they joyful? Were they perplexed? Were they annoyed? These are the kinds of questions we want to wrestle with as we are preparing our sermons.

I had a pastor in college whom I loved dearly. Every single week the mood or tone of Pastor Tom's sermon was one of yelling. He yelled all the time. It didn't matter if he was preaching a joyful, encouraging sermon or a sermon of correction and rebuke. It was always the same mood—yelling. And what happens when we listen to a sermon that doesn't match the text is that we start scratching our heads. We wonder, *Is that truly how God feels about me all the time? Is that really what God wants to have me do in my life? Is He really encouraging when He's angry? Or is He angry when He's encouraging?* We can really confuse our listeners when our vocal variety—the pitch, pace, and punch—do not match the mood of the text.

As we are sitting in our studies, praying and plowing through the text, we're trying to understand it, we're trying to grapple with it, with the idea and the various sub-points of the text. But one of the things we can forget is to think about the mood of the text. So as you're in your study this week, as you're preparing that sermon for this coming Sunday, I want you to match the mood of the text. Allow the text to dictate your sermon's mood and allow that mood to follow you into the pulpit. Match the mood of the text.

Give your listeners the opportunity to respond to the message

9

SMG

When we preach, we want to make an impact on our listeners. That is our goal. We are not the ones who make *the* impact; God ultimately does. But when we think about the conclusion of the sermon, and as we bring it to an end, we want to give our listeners an opportunity to respond to the message. How do we do that? Once we have landed the plane with the conclusion, what can we do in order to help our listeners reflect and respond to the message? In a lot of churches, what happens immediately after a sermon is that a hymn or song is announced and, in some places, an invitational hymn is given and the listeners have an opportunity to respond by sitting in their seats and praying or even coming to the front of the sanctuary and bowing in prayer and praying with the elders or the deacons or the pastor. There are various ways that we could conclude our sermons by enabling our listeners to have an opportunity to respond to what has been preached.

One way is that we could simply allow a time of prayer. We could lead in a thoughtful prayer with our listeners about the sermon itself, the idea, the purpose to which we have been moving. It is not a prayer in which we would re-preach the sermon. (For example, "O Lord, we thank you (1) that you are a wonderful God; (2) that you are a gracious God"—not that.) This is a prayer that thoughtfully brings our listeners to the place where the sermon's purpose is hit.

Another type of prayer is a time of silence where the listeners can reflect on and respond to the sermon. Here the pastor can lead listeners by suggesting items for them to pray about as they spend time in silence. This time of prayer might also be a responsive prayer, a prayer that you as the pastor and the worship team have put together that encapsulates the goal of the sermon itself.

In addition to prayer, different kinds of music might be used to accomplish the sermon's purpose. It may be a choir, an ensemble of some sort that will sing a reflective type of song that is in tune with the message itself. It may be a soloist, someone who sings gently, or somebody who plays the guitar, or some instrumentalist who plays a flute or a violin, or some type of music that enables listeners to respond to the message. The hymn or a worship song can reflect the intent of the sermon itself.

Prayer. Music. Also include confession—a time of confession, a confession led by the pastor or worship leader, a written out confession whether in the worship bulletin or on the screen where the congregation can respond to the message in a thoughtful way as they consider God's Word and the impact it has on their lives. It might be that you would want to allow the listeners to have some time to write on their worship folder some suggestions of ways in which they could put the message into practice themselves or suggest some action for them (writing a note or letter or enabling them to have opportunity to speak to those who are seated around them—reflecting the intent of the message).

Whatever it might be, our goal in preaching is to see that what we are speaking about is applied to and has an impact on our listeners. So when we think about what it means to conclude a sermon and see what happens after the sermon, we want to do this: Give your listeners the opportunity to respond to the message.

Make preaching a priority

HWR

If God has given you the opportunity to be a leader in your local church, then one question you have to ask is, What are my priorities? What do I have to put first, second, and third in my life?

I think many people would agree that these are great questions but they haven't answered them well. Being the pastor of the church is so demanding—you have to be a communicator, counselor, board member, evangelist, etc. You have more than you can do. I would like to suggest that you would be wise to make preaching a priority. Preaching isn't everything but it is essential to an effective ministry.

In a local Protestant church, people assemble once every week or more to hear you preach. They have other associations with you, but preaching is the main one. I'm convinced that a powerful pulpit affects all the other ministries you do. In fact, I suggest that if you have a powerful pulpit, it can take care of other ministries. For example, if you have people in your church who are caught on the barbed wire of life, they can use individual counsel; however, they can also help themselves if they see, from the Scriptures as you preach, what they might do in their difficult situation. If you see yourself being a leader, certainly in your preaching you will articulate a vision for the church. You have a chance to do that from the pulpit in a way that you cannot do in any other situation.

10

Let's face it. We can't be all circumference. We have to have some center. How we minister will depend on what that center is. If it is another center than preaching and you put preaching aside, I think you will suffer for it. Over the years, I have had probably five hundred congregations contact me about a pastor. In all of those situations but two, when I have asked, "What do you want in the person who pastors your church?" the answer was, "We want an effective preacher." In fact, of the remaining two, one church felt it needed someone to be a better leader than the former pastor but their second choice was preaching. In fact, if you think about it, they call you "the *preacher*." That's their way of referring to you and your job. A preacher that doesn't preach is like a clock that doesn't run. It's called a clock and is supposed to tell time but only does so twice a day. It is failing at its center, at the thing it ought to be doing. For the sake of your ministry and for the sake your people, make preaching a priority.

Guard your sermon preparation time

MDK

Have you ever found yourself in the middle of a hospital room? You're holding the hand of a parishioner who is on her final breath. Maybe you're in a PTA meeting at the local elementary school. Perhaps you're listening to the voices of all different people from the community who don't want a shopping mall to enter your town. Maybe you're at a sporting event for one of your kids. On the sidelines you're rooting for her and cheering her on. And as you sit in these different venues, you're thinking, *How am I going to get the sermon done for Sunday?* There are so many things that vie for our time. Many challenges exist in pastoral ministry. We want to be there for our families, but we also want to be there for our church members. And we want to prepare relevant, faithful, biblical sermons.

I want to encourage you to guard your sermon preparation time. It's not easy to do that. We have so many responsibilities. When I was a pastor in Colorado, there were so many things that factored into the schedule. How could I allocate my time? There are elements of life that come into play that we don't schedule in, such as a funeral or an elders' meeting that goes too long. But sometimes, as Charles Hummel says, we can fall prey to the "tyranny of the urgent." There are so many things that bombard us. We feel pressured to send a quick email back to John who needs our help. Maybe we feel pressed because one of our kids is sick. Again, there are so many life moments that press into our schedules. And one thing that easily gets squeezed out is sermon prep. We just can't seem to find enough time in the day to be able to guard our time.

Jonathan Edwards, a well-known preacher from the Great Awakening era, was known to stand in his home as he prepared his sermons. He would look out onto the fields and see his parishioners working from the sweat of their brows. They would be tilling the fields and preparing the harvest for the enrichment of the entire community. And he would similarly look out and prepare the sermon. As he prepared the sermon, he saw his parishioners working diligently in the fields. And they could see him from his window as he poured his heart into studying the Word of God. There was a symbiotic relationship where they were looking at him and he was looking at them. Both pastor and parishioners were doing God's work. He spent hours and hours and hours, a full day's study, each day pouring his life into God's Word as God poured the Word of God into him. There's something beautiful about that image, where we are working diligently on behalf of the people and they're working diligently for the community and for the kingdom of God. One of the things that we want to guard against is sheer laziness and other activities that can press into our lives in such a way that it leaves sermon prep for the last minute.

When can you prepare a sermon? Really any time that works for you. Maybe you can block out three hours in the morning each day or alternate between mornings and afternoons. Maybe evenings are more conducive for your schedule. No matter when the schedule permits, make time for sermon preparation. It's not easy. There will be moments when we are going to fall prey to the tyranny of the urgent. But if we can build healthy rhythms of sermon preparation into our schedules, it will enrich us and our people. And ultimately, God will be glorified. So guard your sermon preparation time.

Preach the principle

PMB

Tie the specific to the principle. If you don't, you could be in danger of becoming Preacher No-No.

My husband and I have three small boys. The youngest, age 2, calls me Mommy No-No. It's a name that I've come to deserve.

Not long ago, the boys were playing outside. As I helped them out the door, I said, "Be nice to each other." That's the principle: Be nice to each other.

It wasn't long before Jack pushed Sam. I gave a gentle reminder, "Hands to yourself."

A few minutes passed. Sam came to the door howling, "Jack poked me with a stick."

"Jack, what happened?"

His face was downcast. "I poked Sam with a stick."

"What did I tell you?" I asked.

My precise little boy replied, "You said *hands* to yourself. I used a *stick*."

"Ok, no sticks," I huffed.

A few minutes passed and Sam yells, "Jack hit me with a pole."

"No poles!" Now I'm hollering.

I looked into my backyard and all I could see were potential weapons. Everything was a no. I barked out the screen door: "No sticks of any kind or variety; no poles; no pool noodles; no whiffle ball bats or baseball bats — plastic, wooden, or aluminum; no shovels; no rakes; no spades; no snowplow markers that should have been removed three months ago; no hoses." The list goes on and on and I am Mommy-No-No.

I don't want to be Mommy-No-No. I want to elevate the conversation to the principle, but the kids live life in the particular. I struggle trying to balance this in life and I struggle trying to balance this in preaching.

The principle is "Be nice to each other." But after an afternoon in the backyard, the principle has been lost on everyone and I am Mommy-No-No. Let's face it, I can never give enough rules to cover everything. The kids need to see the connection between the rules and the principle. It's really the principle I'm after.

Sometimes, we can be Preacher No-No. We rattle off a list of do's and don'ts. They are rules to be followed. But if the rule is divorced from the principle, then we're headed down the road toward legalism.

When we give a specific, remember to tie it to the principle. "Don't chase your brother with a stick. *Be nice to each other.*" Tie the specific to the principle. It seems so simple, but when we forget the principle, we become Preacher No-No. Preach the principle.

Drain the liquid

JDA

In an issue of *Leadership* journal, Lee Eclov tells the story of a researcher named Hillary Koprowski, who was a leader in the search for the polio vaccine in the 1940s. Koprowski and his team had done animal tests successfully, and the next step involved a powerful but unwritten rule of scientific research: Before testing an oral vaccine on other humans, the researcher must try it himself. So late one winter afternoon in 1948, he and his assistant whipped up a polio cocktail and the two men drank from small glass beakers. They tilted their heads back and drained the liquid fully. They agreed it tasted like cod-liver oil. The assistant said, "Have another?"

"Better not," Koprowski said, "I'm driving."

Lee Eclov says that every preacher has to take the same gutsy step. We have no right to give other people our "holy vaccine" until we've drained the liquid ourselves. And sometimes it does taste like cod-liver oil.

As preachers we must *drain the liquid*. Preach to yourself before you preach to others. Ask yourself, "Am I living the life I'm recommending to others?" "Authenticity" is one of the god-terms of our culture—and rightly so. Of the members of the old rhetorical trio of ethos, pathos, and logos, Aristotle said that ethos is number one. Your character, trustworthiness, experience, and sincerity—your ethos—are the most persuasive tools you possess. So this week and every week when you're doing your sermon preparation, remember to drain the liquid yourself.

13

Interrupt your preaching plan

I4

SMG

"Interrupt your preaching plan" might not sound like the best of ideas, but, as Solomon writes, "There is a season for everything: a time to be born, a time to die . . ." and his list goes on. If that is really the case, then for us as preachers, we want to be ready for when these unexpected occasions pierce into the life of our church. That is, we have put together a plan, and I am all for a plan because it is an important part of what it means to move men and women into maturity in Jesus Christ, because as you look out beyond the next week, the next month, and into the next year, and the next couple of years, you are getting a sense of how you might move people toward growth in Him. That is great. That is fine. That is what we want to do. But, there are occasions, however, where our plan has got to be interrupted. It forces itself upon us, upon the church, the interruption does.

Consider the tragedy of 9/11, the tsunami in Japan, Katrina in New Orleans, international airline crashes, etc. What kind of impact does that have on a church? Depending on where you are especially, it is going to have an impact. These interruptions have the potential of shaping the thinking and shaking the faith of our listeners. As preachers, we want to be ready to deal with these interruptions, for when crisis comes to our doorstep, it doesn't just knock gently; it barges through the door. So as preachers, we recognize that this matter (e.g., a traffic event, a death of a prominent member in the congregation, a death that takes place that is horrific, any kind of crisis that blows through the church) is something that you don't want to ignore.

A friend of mine from New York City attended a local Boston area church following the 9/11 terrorist attack and noted that not once in the entire service did the pastor or other service leader recognize what took place in New York City—not through the prayers, not even in the sermon itself. This is inexcusable. Haddon Robinsons notes, "When we preach well, the steel of God's Word strikes the flint of people's lives." What a tremendous opportunity to help people to see the power of God's Word in a particular situation! So that is why, when we think about our preaching and the preaching plans, we want to be flexible enough to interrupt them because they are worth interrupting. It is that kind of attitude that we want to have that will help our people understand theologically and biblically the world in which they live.

So how do you do this? How do you plan for crises? I wish I could tell you that I have a 1-2-3 step approach to doing so. One thing that we want to do is to be open to changing what we have planned. Then, to be aware of what is going on. Sometimes for us as preachers we are in our own bubble; we live our lives in an atmosphere not necessarily that of our listeners. But if we are pastors shepherding our people, we are going to be aware of the needs and aware of their reaction to different crises, whether it is a financial crisis where the markets collapse, planes that fly into a superstructure, or a tragic death—a child hit by a car. These tragedies have an incredible impact on a church and raise all kinds of questions in members' minds. Our task is to help them to think theologically, to think biblically, and to help them to be able to deal with this tragedy in a Christianly way.

So when we consider interrupting our preaching plan, we want to do so prayerfully, flexibly, and sensitively, so that we can reach the men, women, boys, and girls under our care with the love of a preaching pastor who knows them and knows how to speak to where they are and when and where they need it most. So don't forget, interrupt your preaching plan.

14

I 5   Don't just get feedback, get feedforward

JDA

To improve your preaching, don't just get feedback, get "feedforward." That means to solicit input *before* you preach. Let me suggest three ways for getting feedforward.

First, you might want to join a social group as a way to do audience analysis. For example, you could become part of a reading group at the local library or university. The British pastor John Stott did that for years. His purpose was not only to read good books, but also to gain feedforward. By listening to folks discuss books he got inside the hearts and minds of the people of his community. Some members of the book group were Christian, and some were not, so he used that experience to gauge their level of understanding and agreement with Christian theology, the Christian worldview, and a Christian lifestyle. You might want to join a tennis team, running club, knitting circle, or another social venue that encourages people to talk and listen to one another. You don't have to pump your group with questions or distribute surveys. Just listen.

Another way to get feedforward is to discuss your sermon text with a small group, perhaps your fellowship group. Seek their input: "Should I say this?" "Is this illustration appropriate?" By soliciting input, you don't have to guess about the appropriateness of your material, or hope that you are addressing listeners' questions. You can find out before you step into the pulpit.

A third approach is the use of a sermon-planning team. This is similar to the suggestion above, but it is a standing committee rather than an ad hoc group. It can be composed of laypeople, elders, pastoral staff, or other people of the congregation. I formed a group like this and they would send me illustrations, pray for me, and partner with me so that sermon prep became a communal activity. Moreover, when you enlist others in the creation of your message, you will discover that they listen more attentively.

Give it a try! Don't just get feedback, get feedforward.

16 A wise leader works exercise into his or her schedule

HWR

Do you exercise? If you are watching television or listening to the radio these days, I'm sure you know the importance of exercise. I'd like to underline it for you. I have learned over the years how important it is to exercise. You don't read much about exercise in the Scriptures. I think the reason is that in the ancient world people got plenty of exercise. They didn't have a bus system to take them from place to place. They didn't have a car into which they could hop when they wanted to go down to the library. They walked. They walked. They walked. Life was filled with exercise. That's not true for us today, is it? It's easy to get in the car and go every place or get public transportation. For you, then, it's important to get exercise into your schedule.

If you can, work out in a gym. Find something that you enjoy doing and do it regularly. It has a lot of advantages. First, it has the obvious advantage of helping you control your weight. Exercise and diet is an important part of what you as a leader have to be involved in. Second, I find it also helps reduce tension. All of us live with tension; it builds up as we minister. There is something about working out on machines or going on a long walk that takes the tension away. I recommend it to you. Find a way, each day, to do some exercise.

My wife Bonnie and I exercise every morning. It's something that we do together. Strange how that helps build our relationship! We go to a gym nearby and I work out on the elliptical machines. There isn't a morning when I wake up that I'm eager to do it. But there hasn't been a morning after we've done it that we regret having gone to the gym. I'm not a great example of exercise but you ought to make it a part of your program. Bodily exercise isn't everything but it is something. Therefore, a wise leader works exercise into his or her schedule.

16

17 Lay hold of the Bible until the Bible lays hold of you

SMG

"Lay hold of the Bible until the Bible lays hold of you." These are the words of Will Houghton, former president of Moody Bible Institute. I happened to follow Will Houghton at the church where I served—though not immediately. He had served as pastor of the church from 1918 to 1920. He came to town as a widower, a father with two boys in tow. He was an evangelist, and the church was without a pastor. They invited him to become the pastor and it turns out he fell in love with the church pianist who happened to be the daughter of the richest man in town! After two growth-filled years Houghton left that little town and later went on to become pastor of Calvary Baptist Church in New York City. After that he moved out to Chicago to serve as president of Moody Bible Institute.

Houghton was a man who was committed to God's Word just like many of us. He was ruminating on a passage in Colossians 3:16, "Let the Word of Christ dwell in you richly as you teach and admonish one another with all wisdom and as you sing psalms and hymns and spiritual songs, with gratitude in your heart to God." Preachers, allow the Word of Christ to dwell in you richly. As you prepare to preach, let it dwell in you richly. Lay hold of the Bible until the Bible lays hold of you.

It is this rich, nourishing feeding of the Word, as we study it, understand it, parse it, and prepare to preach it, that we don't want to miss, allowing that Word to dwell in us richly, to change us, to be applied to us. Haddon Robinson says in his definition of expository preaching that preaching is not only to be something that is a historical, grammatical, and literary study of the Word, but this Word also has an impact on the life and thinking of the preacher, even before it is preached. Lay hold of the Bible until the Bible lays hold of you.

17

So often in our rush to prepare sermons, we forget to allow this Word of Christ to dwell in us richly, to take up residence in our souls so that the text we preach isn't something that is communicated only to our listeners but the truth of the text has actually had its opportunity to rule in our lives as well. Yes, Will Houghton was right. I was reminded many times when I was pastoring that little church, "When Will Houghton was here there were many people in the service. When Will Houghton was here we had a large choir." But what I remember from Will Houghton is what he emphasized for me as a young, fledgling preacher: Lay hold of the Bible until the Bible lays hold of you.

I hope that, as we prepare our sermons for our listeners, we will allow that Word of Christ to dwell in us richly and make a difference in our lives, too. I'm sure you agree with Will Houghton: Lay hold of the Bible until the Bible lays hold of you.

18   Use your introduction to set up the body of the message

HWR

In my lifetime I have listened to, I suppose, more than a thousand sermons. Many of them have been the fledgling sermons of new preachers in a homiletics class, but others have been sermons of people who have been around the block a while. One of the things I have had to wrestle with is that some sermons are clear and other sermons are not. I can't imagine that anybody begins to preach by saying, "This Sunday, my aim is to be confusing. I'm really going to try to lose the listeners and somehow make them think I'm profound." I think most of us want to be clear in what we preach. So the question is, "What can we do to increase clarity?"

I'd like to focus on just one thing that seems so obvious but we often miss. That is, a good introduction gets attention and it surfaces need; but then that introduction *goes into the body of your message*. There is no such thing as a good introduction. There is only a good introduction of a particular message. I'm surprised how often we go from the introduction into the body of the message without being sure that the people who listen realize there is a bridge between the introduction and what follows. I've seen students, again and again, do a good job with the introduction in the sense of getting my attention and making me sense that there is a need for this, then, suddenly, they are into the sermon and have never built the bridge. I've seen that happen with the people that should know better.

The assumption is that people will know how our introduction relates to our body of the message and that is not a good assumption. I have to take time to make the connection. I have to take time, at least, to raise the subject of the message (i.e., what exactly am I talking about?) and not just in a vague way (e.g., "Today I want talk about money"), but in a specific way (e.g., "I want to talk about why we should give our money or how we should handle our money"). You build that by coming from an introduction that raises that need. Then, you state the subject. You restate it—you go back and say it again. Then, you move into the body of the message, either to the major idea of the message or to the first major movement of the message.

So if you want to be clear each week as you preach, at least ask, How does my introduction relate to the body of my message? And if you find that out, tell your listeners. Don't keep it a secret. One thing you can do for clarity is use your introduction to set up the body of the message. That takes thought. It takes work. It takes good transition. But if you do it, your sermon has a better chance of being clear. It's sage advice: Use your introduction to set up the body of the message.

19   The essence of good preaching is unity, order, and progress

HWR

Sometimes when people think about preaching, they think about a bunch of rules (i.e., there are three things that go into an introduction; the ways in which you make a good outline; if you are going to use illustrations, you ought to have one for every point). Those are the kinds of rules you get. Those rules don't answer a basic question: What is the essence of good preaching? The rules get at the essence. I have taught preaching for a number of years and I suggest the essence of a good sermon is that it has unity, order, and progress. Many of the rules try to get you to that, but you can forget the rules if the sermon has unity, order, and progress.

We talk about unity. We are talking about many things that are not seen before being together, coming together, or things that were not together before but we're bringing them into harmony with one another. Every great work of art has unity. Every great piece of music has unity. Every play has unity — it has scenes, it has acts, but it comes together — it is one out of many. That is what is in the back of our coins and is what ought to be in the back of our minds. A sermon has unity. The thing about the unity that we have as we preach is that, unlike a picture which we can look at, whole and complete, and see its oneness, the sermon is a unity conveyed in time. It starts at 11:25 and ends at 11:50. And, we have to give it a piece at a time. So that makes it a bit more like a great symphony. You hear one note before you hear another note, but then you hear the whole symphony and you feel the unity. That makes it like a play—you can't see it whole and complete at one time. You ought to see a sermon as unity before you preach. You ought to see the whole thing. Then you take it apart. So a good sermon has unity.

A good sermon also has order. That comes out of the fact that a sermon is a unity conveyed in time. I need to give the listener the piece that the listener needs when the listener needs it. Then, as I am working, I need to show the listener how the piece I am giving to her or to him now is connected to the pieces I have just given her or him. Listeners can't think for themselves. They are sitting there listening to you. If they start thinking, *How does this fit? How does this point go with what he said?* they forget what you are saying. You've got to show them. You've got to go back. You've got to review. You've got to show them the order of your message. So order is a way of putting the unity, conveyed in time, together. Good sermons have that.

Good sermons also have a sense of progress. They are going someplace. A conclusion ought not to be left to the last minute before you get into the pulpit or, even worse, after you are in the pulpit hoping somehow this thing is going to end. Good communication is going someplace and you can sense it even in the introduction. You can sense that this preaching has a destination in mind. Some sermons slog it out and the preacher quits because it is almost twelve o'clock. My father was not a very sophisticated person but he listened to a lot of sermons and time to time he would say, "Well, it was all right, but he had five good stopping places and didn't take any of them." A good sermon doesn't have five good stopping places. It ends when the preacher is through. If you preach for twenty minutes and you are through, then stop. Some Sundays you may have to go thirty-five minutes and then stop. But a congregation knows that you quit when you're through, when you get to your destination you stop.

Three things that a sermon has—all the rules get at those three things or they are not worth talking about—unity, order, and progress. The essence of good preaching is unity, order, and progress. If you can work on those, you'll have the essence of great communication.

19

Diversify your illustrations

MDK

I once sat under the preaching ministry of a pastor who loved his people. He cared about them. Everyone knew it. Everyone felt it. But after years of listening to his sermons, it was overtly clear that his illustrations came primarily from one source: quotations. He would share lengthy quotes from his favorite preachers, famous pastors, and other well-known people. Those quotations served as the source of his illustrative material. He seldom deviated from using quotations. Now there's nothing wrong with using quotations. They can really shine light into a particular moment. Those exact words need to be expressed. But we know that illustrations could use some diversifying. I want to encourage you to diversify your illustrations.

Illustrations do primarily three things. They function to explain, prove, or apply, as Haddon Robinson explains in *Biblical Preaching*. Some concepts need to be explained. Therefore, we're going to use an illustration that explains the text. Sometimes we want to persuade our listeners. We want to prove that the biblical concept or event actually occurred and validate its accuracy. So in those moments, we want to persuade or prove. To do so, we might tell a story from life to bolster persuasion. Lastly, we want to apply the text. We want to help listeners put into practice exactly what is being taught. So we find an illustration from life that applies the concept.

Now where do we get illustrations? Illustrations can come from any source. You can think of personal examples. Think of the moment when you were driving down the highway and someone cut you off. Share with your listeners the things that you wanted to say, but couldn't say or didn't say. Give them examples of showing restraint in a moment of anger or frustration. You can think of a story that you tell your children at bedtime. Stories are powerful ways to illustrate what we're trying to communicate. We can also use movie clips with discernment. Sometimes a clip from a movie will convey what we're trying to communicate in the sermon. We can create hypothetical situations. We can find them in newspapers or by observing people and how they interact with one another. Illustrations can come from statistics or novels.

Simply put, illustrations can come from any source when we use our creativity. Instead of relying on one form alone, diversify your illustrations. Find creative ways to illustrate your points as you explain, prove, and apply the text. Diversify your illustrations.

20

HWR

I was involved with a study some time ago in which we asked several hundred preachers, "What is the most difficult part of the sermon for you, the part of the sermon you don't think you do very well?" The answer we got was "conclusions—we really don't do conclusions well." Teaching the Doctor of Ministry program at Gordon-Conwell, I've asked people in our class, all of whom are pastors, "What part of the sermon do you think is your weakest?" And again they say, "It's the conclusion." I've wondered about that. I've wondered why conclusions tend to be weak. They ought to be one of the things we emphasize.

In communication, there is the law of primacy and there is the law of recency. The law of primacy says that the *first* things we say in our sermons are the most important (i.e., people remember them the most). Introductions really can set you up for a good sermon. But the law of recency says that the *last* thing you said, the most recent thing you said, is what people will tend to remember. Granting that those studies are valid (I think they are), then the law of recency is the law that says, "Work on your conclusions." I think we know that. But I think the reason that we don't do it is that we tend to work on our introductions, move our way through a sermon, and as we get it down and start to mumble it, we get through almost all of it and something happens (e.g., your spouse wants you to take out the garbage or someone is at the study door). So we start over and go through the sermon again. We start at the beginning, go through it, and hope that when we get on our feet Sunday morning something will happen and that will allow us to have a conclusion.

I've heard sermons—I've preached them—that resemble the airplanes circling Logan Airport in Boston. Imagine it. It's a tough day. The planes are going to land. They come in. Then, before they land, they take off again. They swirl around, come down, get almost in, and then go out. I've heard sermons like that. They swirl around and hope somehow that they will land well. I don't think you can risk that. You're wise as you work on your sermon if you understand what your central idea is and what the purpose of the sermon is and sketch out a conclusion. It will be rough. You can work on it later, but that conclusion is saying, "This is where I'm going. This sermon is going for that airport." If you do that, you'll find that it concentrates you. It helps you to have a sense of progress in your message. It's going someplace.

Many times we can preach sermons that are strong but end weakly. You don't want to do that. The law of recency says put time in your conclusions. That's the reason you are preaching the sermon. That's the place in which you show people how to put your truth in action. That's the thing that drives it home to a burning focus in people's minds. After all, isn't that what we are trying to do? Take the truth of the Bible and drive it home to a burning focus in people's minds. If they get it, there is a better chance that they will put it to work in their lives. Yes, conclusions should come to a burning focus.

It doesn't all depend on you

SMG

In preaching, it doesn't all depend on you. For most preachers, this is good news, that is, that our preaching is not solely based on our study, our background, the way we communicate, or even the congregation—the place in which we speak. Really, it's all about God. We have heard it said that it is all about God. It *is* all about God. All that we do, all that we have, all that we attempt to do is about God. The act of preaching itself is an act of worship. So what we do as we worship, as we preach, as we communicate God's Word to God's people, we do all that we have been required to do (i.e., we work with the text, pray, understand our listeners, exegete them, prepare a sermon that is clear and concise, and communicate God's Word to them) and then we leave the rest up to God. We give it to God as an act of worship. Preaching is not dependent solely on us. That really is good news. It does not all depend on you as a preacher.

For a lot of us who struggle in contexts where we think people are not hearing what we have to say, we may find out that weeks or years later that what we said and how we said it was something that has been a keen insight and an encouragement for growth for somebody, because it all doesn't depend on us. And yet, as preachers, we know that we don't give up the responsibility of doing all the work that we have to do—the study that we are called to do—because of all the gifts that

God has given to us. But that is it isn't it? It is God who gives gifts. It is God who has given us His Word. It is God who does His work.

22 There is a mystery to preaching that I do not quite understand, because once we stand up to deliver God's Word, it is set on the hearts of the people. When that happens, as we have prayed that God would work, the flint of God's Word strikes the steel of people's lives as Haddon Robinson says, some kind of spark takes place, and God does His work. So be encouraged, preachers. Be encouraged to know that the work that you do (i.e., the study that you do, the way that you stand and communicate to a congregation that you have understood and have tried to intersect with as you clearly communicate God's Word to them) is well worth doing. It is assuring for us to know that God is the one who does the work. It is true. It is encouraging. It is freeing as well. In preaching, it does not all depend on you.

Preach as a dying man to dying men

23

JDA

"I preached as never sure to preach again, as a dying man, to dying men." You may have heard this statement before. It's from Richard Baxter who wrote the Puritan classic *The Reformed Pastor*. He is telling us that every time he stepped into the pulpit he recognized that it could be his last sermon—one day it was. Baxter also recognized that it could be the listener's last sermon—one day it was. The conviction of human mortality and the brevity of life drove him to speak clearly, with pastoral warmth, as one who kept watch over the souls of his people.

The Bible uses various metaphors for the brevity of life: We are a shadow that passes. The span of our days is a handbreadth. We are like grass that springs up in the morning but then withers in the afternoon. We are as thin as vapor. We preach to dying men and women.

Baxter understood the brevity of life because he was a pastor. The minister who marries, buries, baptizes, and counsels lives with the awareness that life is brief. So Richard Baxter tells us to consider human mortality—ours and that of our listeners—to ignite our passions as we stand to teach the Word. Meditate on the brevity of your days so that you can preach like Richard Baxter: "as never sure to preach again, as a dying man, to dying men."

24 Be yourself when you preach

HWR

This seems almost obvious; but when you stand up to preach, be yourself. Years ago when I first began preaching, the models I had were people who were orators. These were the kinds of folks who were featured at conferences and they would have a sense of speaking to the ages. So I copied them. I remember that after I had been preaching for about a year, a friend of mine who came to hear me said, "You know, it is interesting. When I talked to you on the way out here in the car, you talked one way. When you got up to preach, you talked another way. You are somebody else in the pulpit. You are not the person that I talked to in the car." I thought about that and I think I began to change to try to be more of myself. When it really came home to me was when I was general director of the Christian Medical Dental Society. I spoke to groups of physicians and dentists. They are a tough audience. They don't give you a lot of response. You give them your best joke and they show you two teeth. But I discovered that I could not have a strong, declarative way of talking at them. I had to talk with them. I had to interact with them in the way I spoke, in the way I tried to get stuff across. I discovered that they wouldn't put up with somebody who was a phony, who was one thing when he stood in front of the group and another when he was interacting with them personally.

I don't think you can afford it. Be yourself when you preach. Be your best self—this is not a plea for sloppiness, for the use of slang, or the use of bad language—but be yourself. Ultimately, what people hear is not a sermon, not an outline. They hear you. So when you stand to speak, help people understand. You'll be intense because you would be intense if you were speaking across a table to somebody. Don't be afraid to laugh because you would do that if you were talking to somebody in your office. Don't make someone else an idol in your life. God made you *you*. There has never been another person just like you, with your background, with your approach to life, with the things that you have seen and done. Be the same person in the car, at home, and in the pulpit. Therefore, since God has made you you, be yourself when you preach.

24

25 Mobilize your language and send it into battle

JDA

It was said of Winston Churchill that "he mobilized the English language, and sent it into battle." I exhort you, send your best words into battle against the world, the flesh, and the devil. Send language forth like soldiers massing for the charge, cutting the wire, and storming the stronghold. You can do this by using vivid verbs and nouns. Don't say, "There was a major city"; say, "Chicago." Don't say, "The thief brought a weapon"; say, "knife," "lead pipe," or "sawed-off shotgun." Don't say, "The devil is all over the place trying to mess up our lives"; say, "he prowls like a roaring lion seeking someone to devour."

Are you familiar with the story of the dramatist who received a package from a budding playwright? The young author had sent a poorly written play and a wordy, pretentious letter: "Sir, I would like you to read the enclosed script carefully and advise me on it. I need your answer at once, as I have other irons in the fire."

The dramatist wrote back, "Remove irons, insert manuscript." Vivid, terse, and direct.

In *Preaching That Connects*, Mark Galli and Brian Larson offer this exercise. See how many words you can cut from this flaccid sentence: "The relentless creativity of God has affected my life in such a consistent manner that I'd like to share with you what I am learning at this point." Maybe you could say it this way, "God's relentless creativity has affected me consistently. Here's what I've learned." The improved example trims the fat. It mobilizes the English language and sends it into battle. Yes, mobilize your language and send it into battle.

25

26   The better you know yourself, the better you can serve God in the situation in which God has placed you
HWR

Let me ask you a question: "Who are you?" It is easy to answer that question by telling me what you do. You are the pastor of the First Episobapterian Church. Or it is possible to answer that question in terms of relationships. You are the husband to your wife, the father to your children, the wife of your husband. Or it is possible to answer that question in terms of your academic progress. You have a degree from college, a degree from a seminary. All of those are adequate answers, but let me ask the question again. "Who are you?" That is a crucial question to answer because, when you stand to speak, *you* are the one who speaks. The congregation doesn't read an outline. They don't have a manuscript. They don't even hear a sermon. They hear *you*. What they think about you, what they think about your integrity, what they think about your honesty—all of that—is important. So when I ask, "Who are you?" it is a fundamental question for a good communicator.

But who are you? If you don't answer that question clearly, you can do a lot of damage to a congregation. We can do it in our preaching, can't we? When we study the Bible, *we* study the Bible. I am convinced that different people read the Bible in different ways. I have some good friends who are African American. I discover that when they read the Scriptures, they see things in the Bible I hadn't seen. They recognize that there are people of God who are held in slavery, but they gain their victory through trust in God. They can point that out all over the Bible. I might not have seen it, but they do. They know who they are in the sense that they are Christians who are African Americans who have had a history. That affects how they read the Bible. It affects how we handle conflict. If you grew up in a home in which you've avoided conflict, you didn't want to face it, and you carry that into your ministry, it can cause you and your family a great deal of pain. For some people it is very hard to do; it is hard to deal with conflict, because they have not had any models in their home for doing it. So, the question is: "Who are you?"

26

I answer that question as a man who grew up in New York City. My mother died when I was a boy. All of that has had an effect on me and it affects the way I think. It affects the way I read the Bible. It affects the way I preach. But being aware of it keeps me from playing to it. So that's the question: "Who are you?" The better you know yourself, the better you can serve God in the situation in which God has placed you.

27   Feed my lambs, not feed my giraffes

SMG

Charles Haddon Spurgeon is known for saying, "Feed my lambs, not feed my giraffes." That's a good maxim for preachers to remember and to think about: *Feed my lambs, not feed my giraffes*. There is a lot of space between the face of a lamb and the face of a giraffe. What Spurgeon is saying, and what he is encouraging all preachers to consider, is the importance of making clear to our listeners what the text has to say.

Billy Graham puts it another way. He says, "Put the cookies on the lower shelf." It's not as if the cookies were bad cookies. They are cookies that are enjoyable, and sweet, and delicious, but they are sure hard to reach when they are up on the shelf that is high, out of the reach of the desired cookie eater. So when we are preaching, we want to be able to help our listeners understand what's said.

Some may criticize that we are dumbing down the Bible. It is thoughtless of us not to take into consideration our listeners if they cannot understand what we are saying.

I remember one pastor who lived in the area where I was living at the time. He was highly educated and people flocked to his church. "We just love to go to Pastor So-And-So's church. We don't understand what he says, but we sure like being there!" I couldn't believe it! For them, they were lambs, but he was feeding the giraffes. He wasn't putting the cookies on the lower shelf. In many ways, what we're doing as pastors and as preachers is taking those little lambs and putting them on our shoulders, enabling them to reach what we have to teach so that they can be strengthened and nourished in their souls.

How can we put the cookies on the lower shelf? To feed our lambs? One way is to remember to whom we are speaking. We are not speaking to our seminary professors or to our seminary classmates. We want to remember that we are talking to regular people who don't have the insight and depth into the Scriptures that we have—and we are to be able to teach as leaders of God's church. If we are able to teach, we are able, then, to feed the lambs, to feed them from the lower shelf. That means the abstractions with which we deal, the technical kinds of concepts that we engage in our exegesis, are not beyond their ability to understand; but it takes our ability to recognize who they are so that we can make it clear to them on their level. Charles Haddon Spurgeon is right. He is right because it is a reminder for all preachers, as we deal with the intricacies of any book or any text. Spurgeon's words are sage, "Feed my lambs, not feed my giraffes."

27

28   Preach to the outer edges

PMB

I preached on five verses in the first chapter of Mark's Gospel. In verses 40–45, Mark tells us about a man who lived on the outer edges of society. He was stuck away from the community, covering his head and yelling out "unclean, unclean." He was not allowed to live within the community. His disease made him unclean. And anyone who came in contact with the leper would also be considered ceremonially unclean. In fact, in ancient times it was believed that leprosy was the result of some vile, hidden sin. Leprosy, it was believed, was a God-given punishment. He was stuck outside, on the outer edges. Can you imagine kids at night, going to bed and hearing off in the distance, the haunting chant of the leper, "unclean, unclean"? The image in their minds would have been one of a monster—someone who had done terrible things and as a result, his face, his body, was disfigured and distorted. This man was stuck outside, on the outer edges.

I started to wonder, as a preacher, did I consider the people on the outer edges? In our congregations, they're not lepers. So who are they?

I think most preaching is aimed at the people in the middle. The brunt of the message hits them and some of it trickles over to the extreme edges—the youth and the elderly. But most weeks, the people in the middle are served up a main course and the outer edges often get the sides—potatoes or pilaf. The message spills over to them, but not in a direct, practical kind of way. Today, I want to think about preaching to the outer edges—preaching to the outer edges in a way that allows them to feast.

Because I think there are kids, there are young people, who feel like they live life on the outside, looking in. Like the leper, they've been pushed to the outer edges. There's life and laughter and a whole world around them, but they are outside of it—not part of it. Maybe they're on the outside because someone else has pushed them there; maybe they're on the outside because they don't know how to get into the community; maybe they're on the outside because of something they said, or the way they dress or the way they look, or because of what they can or cannot do. But I am certain that every kid, at one point or another, knows what it's like to be on the outside, looking in.

And I imagine that the elderly among us also know what it's like to be outside, looking in. Maybe it's new ideas and fresh faces that have pushed them outside; or maybe lack of mobility or loss of hearing or sight has pushed them to the outer edges. Maybe it's serious illness that has pushed them outside. Or maybe they're on the outside because of something they said, or the way they dress or the way they look, or because of what they can or cannot do. But I imagine that many of our oldest folks know what it's like to be on the outside, looking in.

Jesus cared for the people on the outer edges. Mark tells us that Jesus reached out and touched the leper. Imagine what that felt like for this man. When was the last time someone reached out to touch him? When was the last time someone looked him in the eye, instead of shielding their eyes from him? This wasn't a one finger poke, or a brush of the skin. Jesus pressed his fingers against the man's deformed body.

My husband was talking to a woman at work who had just lost her mother. She said to him, "I miss her. I miss the way she feels. I wish I could hug her." After that, I had a little meeting with my mom and dad. They are a big part of my life. I see them five days a week. My dad comes over every morning and feeds Tim while I get Jack and Sam off to school. My mom and dad come back later in the day if I need to run errands or go to work for a few hours. If we have a meeting or Bible study at night, they come back. In this little meeting I said, "We're going to start hugging. Every time you leave, we'll hug." There are some days that I hug my parents ten times. It's funny now, but that human contact is important.

Do you know there are people—especially the oldest among us—who have not had meaningful physical contact in years? The squeeze of a hand, a hug from a son or daughter, the stroke of fingers through the hair. There are kids, who are on the outer edges; sometimes they seem so distant and unapproachable, but what would they give for an embrace overflowing with love and compassion? Once a child reaches age seven, particularly boys, physical contact by parents decreases dramatically.

Jesus touched the leper. He cares for people on the outer edges.

When you preach, consider the people on the outer edges. Let them know that God's touch can be felt in the most outer reaches. In the loneliest, most desolate places, God's touch is present. In the situation where it seems nobody can help—God can reach it. It's not too far for His touch. Preach to the people on the outer edges; they need God's touch.

In our preaching, less is more

HWR

There is an old story that preachers tell: A man came to church one Sunday and the only person who was there, besides himself, was the preacher. The preacher was hesitant to preach his sermon to one man sitting in the front row, but the man said, "Look, I came to church and I expect that you preach. I need to be fed." So the preacher got up and preached his sermon and he got caught up in the moment. When he was through and on the way out, he stood at the door. This one listener shook his hand and said, "That was good, preacher. But I was the only person there and I want you to know if I have one cow, I don't give them the whole load of hay." Basically what he was saying was, "You fed me too much." By the way, that would've been true if there had been one hundred people there.

As I have reflected on preaching, it strikes me that *less is more*. When I got out of seminary, I thought *more* was more. I thought the essence of preaching was to give everything in the passage and give it all the same kind of weight. As a result, my sermons were weighty and heavy but they were not good communication. A while ago, I was looking at a sermon I preached thirty years ago on Ephesians 5. That is the passage that begins by talking about husbands and wives, goes on to talk about parents and children, then servants and masters. I preached the whole thing — 25–30 minutes — I preached the *whole* thing.

I can't imagine doing that today. I think if I were going through that passage and I came to the admonition, "Fathers, provoke not your children to wrath, but bring them up in the nurture and the admonition in the Lord," I would preach a sermon on that. You've got all kinds of questions you have to answer:

· Why was this addressed to fathers and not mothers?
· How do you provoke your children to wrath? What do you do to make your kids angry?
· Do fathers do that more than mothers? (I think they do, but you have to think about it.)
· Why does provoking them to wrath keep me from bringing them up in the nurture and the admonition of the Lord?
· What does "the nurture and the admonition in the Lord" mean? Parents have admonitions (e.g., Bring in your bike! Go to bed! Eat your food!) But what does it mean when you say, "the admonition of the Lord"?

That's one verse! But if I could get that across on a Sunday morning to many congregations and help them to see what that meant, it would be a good sermon. In fact, it would be far better than starting in Ephesians 5 and going all the way through Ephesians 6. Somebody has said that people come to church and need to be fed, so give them a loaf of bread—don't give them a wheat field. I've come to the place in life where I think I'd do better if I give them a good slice of bread, covered with jam, and see to it that they enjoyed it and ate it. I believe less is more. Don't give them the whole wheat field. Give them a loaf of bread, maybe even a slice of bread, based in the Scripture, which indeed is the bread of life to the people to whom you are preaching. In our preaching less is more.

JDA

Remember ERP: Estimated Relationship Potential. This is a social science theory from the field of interpersonal communication which demonstrates that when we meet someone we quickly form an estimate of the potential for a relationship. We start to calculate: *What kind of relationship is possible here? What will the nature of our relationship be? Will it be a romantic relationship? Will it be an authoritative relationship? Maybe I want to avoid this person.*

Most of this process of estimation is done subconsciously. It is based on factors such as physical appearance, dress, facial expression, accent, and vocabulary. We try to determine if the person is similar or dissimilar to us and whether or not we could connect with him or her in a meaningful way.

Even though ERP is a theory from interpersonal communication, it applies to public ministry. When you stand up to speak, people subconsciously estimate the kind of relationship they can expect. This is especially true for visitors who are seeing you in the pulpit for the first time. It is also true for long-time church members. Every Sunday they form an estimate of what each particular sermon will be like.

So ERP tells preachers to start well. Be yourself, don't mimic another preacher, but begin your sermon with energy, a smile, and good posture. The first sixty seconds of your sermon set a tone and influence how people will respond to the rest of the sermon.

ERP also tells us to choose and train the greeters and ushers of our churches with care. The volunteers who hand out the bulletin or shake hands at the door set an expectation for the entire Sunday experience even if the initial contact takes only seven seconds.

ERP also counsels us to walk about the church property to scrutinize its visual aspects. Start in the parking lot and use the eyes of a visitor as she approaches your church. Is it clean? Is it well marked? As folks walk up to the church, they are exercising ERP, Estimated Relationship Potential. Remember the ERP Factor.

Preach "we" more than "you"

MDK

Preach "we" more than "you." What do I mean? A lot of times when we preach, we often use the pronoun "you." And what that does, is that it separates us from our listeners. Let me give you an example. I was playing basketball with one of my church members. During our fierce battle on the court, he stopped and said rather nonchalantly, "Matt, it must be hard for you."

"What do you mean?"

He replied, "You have to be holy, but I don't have to. Your life must be pretty hard."

I was taken aback a little by that comment. But what he meant is that pastors can sometimes be elevated in the minds of listeners. For some congregants, there is still some degree of reverence and respect for pastors. It has the potential of putting up a wall between us and our people. One of the ways that we can combat this is to use the pronoun "we." It means that I'm part of the message. I'm one of the participants in the sermon. Using "we" demonstrates that the sermon isn't just for my listeners. It's for me as well.

The prophet Micah in chapter 3 scribes these words, "Then I said, 'Listen, you leaders of Jacob, you rulers of the house of Israel. Should you not know justice, you who hate good and love evil?'" There's a tone to this text. There's a sense of otherness, that the prophet is different from the people. And yes, there is a place for that. Absolutely! There are times when we are to rebuke and challenge in love and exhort our listeners to obey God's Word. At the same time, we want to recognize that there is a sense of shared community. Just because I'm a preacher doesn't mean I'm not a participant in the life of the congregation. We're in this together. Haddon Robinson writes, "At that point [of application], it's appropriate for the preacher to leave behind 'we' in favor of 'you.' No longer is the preacher representing the people to God; he is representing God to the people." Therefore, one of the ways that we can really help our listeners is to establish a sense of rapport by simply using the pronoun "we."

Using "we" eliminates distance from our listeners. When we stand behind a pulpit, it creates a natural barrier. Similarly, when we're elevated physically in some sanctuaries, we're literally looking down on our listeners. But one of the ways that we can eliminate that sense of space and distance between us and the listener is to use the pronoun "we." It also helps with vision casting. When we give a concrete vision for the church, we might say, "*You* have to do this. *You* have to be the people of God. *You* have to serve the poor. *You* have to do all these things." But when we use the pronoun "we," it helps us connect. We're saying, "I'm not just the person in command who tells you what to do. I'm in this with you."

Preaching helps us see ourselves in the story. We're also participants in the kingdom of God and in God's work collectively. We're not just telling people what they ought to do. We're in the trenches with them. We love them. We serve them. We're in this together. So one of the things we can do in our preaching to help us connect with our listeners better is to include ourselves in the sermon. Why not try it when you preach? Preach "we" more than "you."

Study your listeners

32

SMG

Study your listeners. Get a sense as to who the people are who are in front of you. Maybe you are going to a new church and you may think, *What I can do is sail along here for a while and pull my sermons out of the barrel and preach them.* But the sermons might completely miss those to whom you speak. The preaching might pass them by because what you have to say does not connect with who they are and where they are—where they are in their spiritual lives, where they are in their lives in general.

We spend a lot of time studying the text, don't we? But, we spend little time studying those to whom we speak. That's one of the biggest challenges for the preacher—to be aware of the people to whom he or she speaks. It is something that we don't want to pass up, but it is something that we often mess up. We think we can stand in the pulpit, shoot from the hip, give our sermon, and sit down without considering the intersection of the truth of the text as it crosses the lives of the listeners.

So what you might want to do as you prepare your sermon is think of the questions that some of the listeners in your congregation might ask. Select someone from an older age group—an elderly man or woman—someone who is unemployed, one of the youth from the church, a stay-at-home mom or dad from the church and imagine them sitting around your desk. Also, don't forget to include someone who asks hard questions—someone who is disgruntled or a person who doesn't necessarily go with the flow.

All of these people's questions will help you understand how **32** you will say what you have to say. You'll want to understand the backgrounds, even broadly (i.e., the congregational background—what the congregation has gone through in the past twenty-five, thirty, forty years).

I remember going to my first church and asking the clerk if I could look at the minutes of the church from the very beginning. The church was founded in 1851. I paged through the minutes and read through lists of mundane things (i.e., offerings given to missionaries, challenges the church faced, rebuilding after a fire). It was in the late 1940s to early 1950s that there was a horrible church split. That church split fractured relationships well into the 1980s when I was still there as pastor. So think about those kinds of factors that make up your listeners—historically, geographically, economically—the issues that people face (e.g., unemployment, factory closings, stimulus like new businesses, health concerns, fractured families, etc.). These things matter when we sit down to prepare to preach. When we sit down to prepare we want to take into consideration those to whom we preach. So it is a good thing because we don't just stand up and preach, we preach to people, real people, our listeners. Study your listeners.

Paper is a poor conductor of heat

33

JDA

Paper is a poor conductor of heat. In other words, it is difficult to generate enthusiasm and passion when reading from a manuscript. May I give you an argument for extemporaneous preaching, an argument *against* preaching with a manuscript? Now before you raise your homiletical red flag and skip what I've written, let me first acknowledge that there are strengths of preaching with a manuscript.

One strength is exact wording. The manuscript allows you to craft your language and carry it directly into the pulpit. Another advantage is exact timing. Preaching from a manuscript removes the guesswork of how long the sermon will last. Another advantage is permanence. The sermon is calcified on paper. One final advantage is comfort, and I suspect that this is the main reason many preachers use a manuscript. It is a safety net under the high-wire act called "preaching."

Having acknowledged the advantages, let me now present my argument against preaching with a manuscript. Quite simply, it is a poor conductor of heat. Very few people write in the same manner as they talk. An oral style of communication has syntactical breaks, redundancies, fragments, rhetorical questions, and other marks of dialogue. Manuscript sermons tend to sound polished, literate, and precise, more like a person is "speechifying" than ministering as a living soul to living souls.

A second disadvantage of preaching with a manuscript relates to delivery. Eye contact, gestures, and movement go down the drain. The manuscript becomes an anchor that limits your movement (or is it a noose?). When we read from sheets of paper (or from the screen of a tablet), most of us sound measured and metronymic. Actual conversation has changes of rate, breaks, hesitations, vocalizations, and sound effects. Very few people read aloud that way when reading from the printed page.

Another argument against preaching with a manuscript is the lack of spontaneity. When everything we wish to say is pre-packaged, measured, groomed, and stage-managed, we hinder our ability to connect with the listener; we lack a *thought-on-fire* quality. Manuscript preaching is often *words-on-ice*.

Finally, let me suggest that using a manuscript may stem from an over-reliance on our own preparation. Of course, I'm not saying you should "wing it." This is not an argument for *impromptu* sermons. Go ahead and write out a manuscript, but don't carry that manuscript into the pulpit because paper is a poor conductor of heat.

MDK

Years ago I sat in a seminary classroom under the tutelage of Dr. Haddon Robinson. He introduced the class to a new book by the late John Stott called *Between Two Worlds*. In this book, Stott describes preaching as bridge-building, that is, bridging the world of the Bible with the world of today. Now, we spend a lot of time thinking about the world of the Bible and all the Bible has to offer about the historical context.

But I want to remind you that effective preachers exegete the Bible and their people. It's critical, of course, that we start our sermon preparation with the Bible. It's from the Bible that we acquire biblical truth that we preach to our listeners. We naturally study the Word. We do our best translation work, do word studies, read commentaries, and gather insights to find the meaning of the text. We determine the central truth from the passage that we're studying. But, frequently, in our sermon preparation, we stop there. We just focus on the world of the Bible, and we forget that we want to be bridge-builders. We want to be the people who stand in the gap and help our listeners understand the biblical world and how it applies to our lives today. Effective preachers exegete the Bible as well as people.

How do we exegete people? What does that mean? It's not like we dissect them in a science laboratory. We're trying to understand who they are and how they think. What are their interests? What are their values? What are their hobbies? What kinds of cultural differences exist among the people in my church? What are their political views? What are the doctrines that hold them captive? We want to understand their world so that we can take biblical truth and accurately apply it to their lives.

I had just begun my senior pastorate in Colorado. A church member came up to me on my first Sunday and said, "On this coming Thursday leave your calendar open. We're going to hang out and have some fun." Immediately my ears perked up as I asked, "What is it that we're going to do?" And he responded, "I'm going to be at your house at 5:00 in the morning. We're going to go wakeboarding together."

Wakeboarding? I thought. *I'm from Chicago. I have no idea what wakeboarding is.*

I must have had a horrific look on my face as he sought to calm my nerves with these words: "Don't worry. Just get up at 5. Be outside ready to go. Make sure you have some swimming trunks and a lot of energy. We're going to have a great time."

So he picked me up at 5 am. We drove for about an hour and got on his boat on the lake. Another church member joined us. They explained the process to me: "Put on this life vest. Get into the water. And basically you're going to ski on top of the water."

I thought, *I've never done this before. How am I going to get up?*

And he said, "Don't worry. The force of the boat is going to push you and you're going to be able to stand up on your feet." As I nervously sat in the ice-cold water, the boat suddenly began to pull my fingers and stretch them. I held on for dear life to a strip of wood. The boat began pulling me and pulling me. I did my best to stand up and for about thirty seconds I stood on top of the water just like they said. I was actually wakeboarding. I was floating across the water until the boat turned. Then I came to a crashing halt and my face planted hard into the water. They laughed at my misery and after a few minutes so did I.

Now, why do I share this story? I share this story because in that moment of wakeboarding, I got to know my new parishioners and ministry partners. I learned about their interests, their values, and their hobbies. I got a sense of their passions in life. I gained knowledge about their desire for Christlikeness and their pursuit for spiritual maturity. I got all that information as we simply joined in an activity that they enjoyed. In that moment, I was unconsciously exegeting them.

As we preach, we want to be able to bridge these two worlds—the world of the Bible and the world of today. I want to encourage you with these words: Effective preachers exegete the Bible and their people.

35 Observant preachers make insightful preachers

SMG

Did you know that observant preachers make insightful preachers? Preachers who are able to observe the world—to understand and reflect on what is going on around them—are insightful preachers. They are able to integrate that which takes place in their own lives and the lives of others with the text and the meaning of a given text. What do I mean by that? There are some people who could go around the world and not really find many insights or illustrations. Yet there are people who could take a walk around the block and observe and see all kinds of things around them.

Several years ago, friends from my home church decided to go on a Caribbean cruise. This was a time when not many people were going on cruises, so when they came back, many of us couldn't wait to see their pictures from their adventure on the high seas. As they laid their photos out on the table, one after another after another did not have in them the beautiful, bright, blue waters of the Caribbean or the white, sandy beaches, nor were there palm trees or other kinds of features of the Caribbean (i.e., dolphins, fish.) No, photo after photo were of the ice sculptures on the ship. Now, I like ice sculptures, but I'm sure the ice sculptures were not the only feature of their trip. They sailed all over the Caribbean and yet what caught their attention were ice sculptures.

Often it is the case that, as preachers, we see ice sculptures rather than a colorful bright world that has relationships and people who enrich it in ways that make it powerful, rich, and, meaningful. What is it that keeps us from being observant and insightful preachers?

Observant preachers pay attention to that which is going on. They listen to conversations. They observe how people interact with each other. They hear the tone of conversation or the manner in which people treat others (e.g., a warm embrace, a cold handshake, flashing eyes). One way you can develop your observation quotient is to go to a mall, sit on a bench, and watch people as they go by. Soon, in your mind, if you start to reflect, you will wonder, *Why is that person walking that way? Why does she limp? I notice the man that is coming toward me is hanging his head, swinging his package back and forth. He looks weighed down.* You hear a conversation of people complaining about their inability to pay their bills. You listen to people correcting their children and how the children speak back and respond to their parents. All of these observations provide a colorful mosaic as to the human condition—what people are like and how they operate.

Years ago, preachers used to have what are called *commonplace books*, that is, empty journal-like books in which they would write down observations about the day. These observations are reflections of how God is working in people's lives and how, at some point, the preacher might integrate these observations into preaching. They might spark illustrations or raise questions. (E.g., "Some of you might be thinking . . . ," and you fill the blank in with a question or statement that is a result of being a good observer of people.)

We want to be able to integrate an observation-like attitude that results in insightful preaching. We cannot help but see how our preaching is influenced by being observant because our eyes are wide-open to the world around us. So if you want to improve your preaching, slow down a little bit and become a more observant preacher as you take in the world around you. It is true: Observant preachers make insightful preachers.

35

JDA

A number of years ago my friend got a new dog, a little puppy named Zebedee. And my friend had a difficult time training Zebedee because he communicated with human speech: "Now, Zebedee, don't do that! You naughty dog, Zebedee! I told you twice! Zebey, I'm warning you!" Zebedee was clueless, and the naughty behavior continued.

So my friend took little Zebedee to dog-obedience school. He discovered that dog-training school is actually master-training school. They taught him how to speak canine with nonverbal cues like body position, eye contact, and tone of voice. That's what dogs understand. So my friend learned cross-cultural communication with his canine.

I tell you that story because when men communicate to women, and vice versa, they experience cross-cultural communication. Men (and women) need to adapt to what the communication scholar Deborah Tannen calls "genderlects."

Let's make some applications to men since they represent the majority of those reading this. Consider the issue of "direction" and "indirection." In American culture, men tend to be more direct than women because they view communication as a means to accomplish a task. But for women, with their high value of smooth interpersonal relationships, communication is a means of communing. They tend to avoid confrontation by leaving the other person options. A conversation might sound like this when Michelle says to Robin, "Do you want to eat somewhere?"

Robin asks, "Are you getting hungry?"

Michelle, "Yeah, a little."

"Me too, do you think we should eat?"

Michelle says, "Sure, sounds good to me. Where do you want to go?"

A man might say, "I'm hungry. Let's eat." But that genderlect would feel brusque or even confrontational to a woman's ears. So men, in your sermon when you apply the truth, try asking questions and making suggestions rather than saying, "If you disobey God, you're an idiot!"

Also consider the art of storytelling. Men tend to tell narratives that deal with competition and/or remarkable action—"The time I went hang gliding!" or "Let me tell you about the weirdest taxi ride I ever had!" Men's stories tend to have a clear conflict and climax. They usually have a punch line or moral at the end. In contrast, women's stories tend to deal with everyday occurrences and may not necessarily lead to a climactic event. To get the feel for genderlects in storytelling, compare a stereotypical guy-movie with a stereotypical chick-flick. So men, when you tell stories, do not neglect everyday experiences like childcare, tension at work, and walking for exercise. Don't forget to adapt to genderlects.

Preach to one person at a time

MDK

Many of us are familiar with the passage in Luke 15. It's the Parable of the Lost Sheep. It goes like this: "Now the tax collectors and sinners were all gathering around to hear him. But the Pharisees and the teachers of the law muttered, 'This man welcomes sinners and eats with them.' Then Jesus told them this parable: 'Suppose one of you has a hundred sheep and loses one of them. Does he not leave the ninety-nine in the open country and go after the lost sheep until he finds it? And when he finds it, he joyfully puts it on his shoulders and goes home. Then he calls his friends and neighbors together and says, 'Rejoice with me; I have found my lost sheep.' I tell you that in the same way there will be more rejoicing in heaven over one sinner who repents than over ninety-nine righteous persons who do not need to repent.'"

What is Jesus talking about in this parable? He's talking about valuing every single person. I want to remind you that we are called to preach to one person at a time.

Now you may say, "Matt, how do you do that? We have thirty, one hundred, three hundred, or five hundred people in the service. How do I just preach to one person?" Haddon Robinson observes, "Life-changing preaching does not talk to people about the Bible. Instead it talks to the people about themselves—their questions, hurts, fears, and struggles from the Bible." A lot of times we can get overwhelmed. There are so many people to consider as we're doing our exegesis and as we're thinking about how we're going to apply this specific passage to their lives. It can be really overwhelming thinking about all the different types of people who are out there. Sometimes, if we're honest with ourselves, we just preach general, generic sermons. We try to hit everyone, but we're not really focusing on any individual.

We can think of preaching as aiming at a target. When you play the game of darts, you're throwing the dart and trying to hit the bull's-eye every time. But one of the ways that we can really focus our preaching on the one sheep that Jesus talks about in this parable is to focus on one individual person. Think of Tom, the software engineer in your church. What are the struggles that he goes through in a given week? What are the questions that he would ask of the particular passage you're preparing your sermon on? What about Jenny, the international student from Ecuador? What is she struggling with? How does she read the text? Perhaps we can think about Mary, the bank teller, or George, who owns the convenience store. What are their situations like? What are the daily struggles that they go through? What kinds of questions do they ask when they read a Scripture passage? How does this text relate to their lives? I knew a pastor who once said that his goal in ministry was this: "to make disciples one person at a time."

Just because we preach to one person and target our exegesis, our outline, our illustrations to that person doesn't mean that we forget about the rest. We're enabling our preaching to home in on an individual so that that individual might be able to sense God's presence and experience all God has for him or her in this passage. I've tried to do this regularly in my preaching. I focus on one individual and ask myself, "How does this text apply to him or her?" It's amazing how God works in that even though I focused on that individual many people in the church benefited from how I preached to that individual.

37

Why not try it in your upcoming sermon series? Think about preaching in this way—to preach to one person at a time.

People-pleasing puts the pulpit in peril

SMG

A lot of us (I am also talking about myself) are people-pleasers. We will do anything to make people like us. We are in the public eye and we are sometimes massaged by the public itself.

When you stand up to preach your listeners are going to make judgments about you. They decide whether they are going to like you or not like you, whether you are organized or not organized, whether you are educated or not educated. They are going to decide whether you are formal or informal. They are going to look at you and make a judgment about whether you are prepared or unprepared. All of these categories are rushing through a listener's mind when a preacher first stands up to preach.

Knowing about these judgments can have a negative effect on preachers. Whether you are in a big church or a small church, you might be pushed around by the church boss or seen as somebody who is anemic in the eyes of the public. The desire, then, to make a name, to make an impression, can drive us in ways that can be perilous.

Some of you might have seen the film *Pollyanna*. The preacher in the film played by Karl Malden is pushed around by Polly, who is the boss not only of the church but also of the entire town. Polly Harrington tells the preacher on what to preach and how to preach it. Then, something happens. Her niece who comes to live with her (i.e., Pollyanna played by Hayley Mills) brings a ray of sunshine into the town and topples things all over the place with her delightful, sunshiny smile and disposition. Karl Malden first resists all of it until Pollyanna falls from a tree and is hurt. Everything begins to make sense to him. He stands up to preach and delivers a sermon unlike any other sermon he has preached, speaking out against the powers of the town, even Polly Harrington.

It is perilous to be pushed around because succumbing to it limits our effectiveness. We really are not our selves; we are somebody else. It blunts our willingness to apply the truth of the text because we are afraid we are going to offend somebody or we are going to hurt somebody. Certainly the truth is powerful. The truth can be painful. But as a preacher, I trust, you are not doing it in a vindictive way. Yet, there are texts that may be offensive to our listeners and we may, because of our unwillingness to deal with the tension in the texts, skip over it, wanting people to like us.

Several years ago I visited a church on the West Coast. The pastor was preaching through the book of Philippians. The Sunday I was there the preacher got to the fourth chapter, where Paul asks the church to straighten out a strained relationship between two women, Euodia and Syntyche. But the preacher skipped that section. In fact, he did not even mention Euodia and Syntyche in his sermon. Maybe he did not want to talk about women. Maybe he did not want to talk about conflict—I don't know. But I sat there and wondered, *Why was this not dealt with?* It could be that some people-pleasing came into play. Maybe there was tension in the congregation. I was baffled.

We are called to be men and women who proclaim God's Word with grace and truth. So be strong in the Lord, in the power of his might. Don't allow what other people think of you to blunt what you have to say—and what the text has to say—and how you live and how you preach God's Word among your people. Love them like Christ. Love them with grace. But remember this: People-pleasing puts the pulpit in peril.

38

Preach to those you want to come

39

JDA

I'd like to pass on some advice I received from Timothy Keller, pastor of Redeemer Presbyterian Church in New York City. Tim says, "Preach to those you want to come to your church and not just those who are there." In particular, preach to unbelievers even if they are not present. That may seem awkward or even foolish, so why does Dr. Keller suggest this?

Because preaching embodies a value system, and by prioritizing seekers, you can set the direction of your church. The *believers* who are present will think, "Wow, this is perfect for Michelle. We were talking about this just the other day." Or, "Guillermo was asking these very questions; I wish he could hear this!" Soon those believers will invite Michelle and Guillermo. But if you preach only to the faithful believers, they may think, "I could never invite Michelle to this." Or, "Guillermo wouldn't understand this." So preach to those you want to come, and eventually they *will* come.

How you do this? Taking a page out of Haddon Robinson's *Biblical Preaching:* We explain, prove, and apply the truth of Scripture. We explain things that are unfamiliar to Michelle and Guillermo. We avoid jargon that only church members know. We also prove. We are apologists, showing the reasonableness of God's claims and commands. And we apply the truth to everyday life. We paint verbal pictures of what the truth looks like when Michelle or Guillermo is interacting with the kids, standing in line at the grocery store, or feeling the stress of being behind schedule on a project.

39 Preach to those you want to come, and watch what the Lord does. He may bring in those very people.

Take a survey of who's listening

40

MDK

In Keith Willhite's book *Preaching with Relevance*, he helpfully writes on the topic of looking from the perspective of the pews. In one chapter he encourages preachers to take a look at preaching from the perspective of the listeners. Who's out there listening to us? I want to remind us to take a survey of who's listening.

Understand your people. Who's out there in that third pew? What makes that person tick? What are his or her interests? What is his or her worldview? How does he or she understand Scripture? To get an accurate picture of how we're to tailor our messages for a particular group of listeners, we want to get to know them. We want to get to know their struggles, ask about their needs, and find ways to connect to their experiences.

Willhite does this is by offering tools to facilitate audience analysis. Generally speaking, what we're trying to do is get a sense of the broad picture of who's out there. What is the demographic of the church? Is there a particular race or ethnicity that is a dominant group? Is it primarily female listeners, or is it an even split between men and women? What are the professions of these listeners? By knowing these facts, we're going to be able to give appropriate application and illustrations to various types of listeners.

Willhite effectively explains different approaches to audience analysis and how we can break it down in our own study. One of the things that he talks about is getting a theological analysis of our listeners by identifying listeners' spiritual conditions. First, there's a group called the "unregenerate." That would be the people who do not know Christ or who may be skeptical of the Christian faith. So take a survey of who's listening. How many people fit into the "unregenerate" category? The second category of people would be "regenerate"—those who actually have a desire for Christ, who know Christ, and who are maturing steadily. Once we get a sense of their spiritual pulse, we're better able to gauge what type of theological doctrines we should concentrate on for a particular message.

In addition, we want to get the age range of our listeners. Find out whether they're in their teens or elderly. What is the financial situation of your listeners? How far do they travel to attend church? What percentage of the listeners is Caucasian, African American, Hispanic American, and Asian American? What percentage of these people are white-collar or blue-collar workers? What percentage of my church is single, married, or divorced? What percentage of my church identifies with a particular political party? Further, we can get a sense of who they are by taking a survey of their educational levels. What percentage of the church has grown up in the church? Many people go to church. They've heard the same messages over and over, but has God's truth sunk into their lives?

Our preaching ministry can be enhanced by knowing who's out there. Who are my listeners? What do they need? What are they hoping for? What do they fear? What are their dreams? These are the types of questions we're asking when we think about taking a survey of who's listening.

Gentleness isn't for wimps

PMB

My kids love superheroes. I'm often asked the question, "Mommy, who is your *favorite* superhero?" Wonder Woman. Of course. A two-inch figure of this female defender stands, ready for action, on my kitchen windowsill. Rounding up criminals with a magic lasso and an icy stare, this woman definitely has what it takes to be a mom. And she does it all in high-heeled red boots. How super-cool is that?

If I were in distress and needed the aid of a protector, I'd call Wonder Woman. But if her invisible jet was in the shop for repairs or the zipper on one of her boots was busted, I wouldn't be disappointed to see Superman, Batman, Spiderman, or Gentle—*or who*? *Gentle*? Wait a minute.

Funny name for a superhero, isn't it? How did that guy get into the hero club? Actually, his real name is Nezhno. Gentle is his nickname, which really makes matters worse. I can understand if "Gentle" was his birth name, given to him by a sweet mother as she held her precious newborn. But this guy earned the nickname Gentle because of his tender demeanor.

I don't know about you, but I'm not sure if I'd trust a superhero named Gentle to get me out of a jam.

But Gentle isn't a wimp. In fact, he's described as one with extreme power—perhaps the strongest in the Marvel Universe. He has super strength, but he detests violence. His massive body is wallpapered in tattoos. These tattoos work to restrain his power. Nobody would call Gentle a wimp. His power is controlled, at bay, tempered.

In Philippians 4:5, Paul says, "Let your gentleness be evident to all."

41

A gentle person shows great restraint. It's a gentle forbearance—an abstaining from the force of a right. The King James Version says, "Let your moderation be known to all." It takes much less self-control to blurt out your demands, or to make a fist, but gentleness requires a thoughtful response. The most challenging time to show gentleness is in the midst of conflict. When there's a disagreement among church leaders or in the family, it's hard to be gentle. And maybe that's because we want to assert our rights. But gentleness puts others before our own rights or our own desires and opinions.

Paul doesn't say, "Let your opinions be evident to all." He says, "Let your gentleness be evident to all."

And he means *everybody*. That's what makes this verse so challenging. It's easy to be gentle to *some* people. But when I'm in the midst of a church conflict, gentleness doesn't come naturally.

But from the pulpit, our listeners should hear a gentleness in our preaching. If you've noticed a harshness or an edge to your preaching, remember that God's Word says, "Let your gentleness be evident to all."

A woman recently confessed that she didn't have a gentle bone in her body. "I'm not sweet," she huffed. "I've never been gentle," she said harshly. Her adult daughter agreed with her mother's self-assessment.

It's true that some people are more naturally inclined toward gentleness than others, but the Bible commands every Christian to let gentleness be evident to all. So how do we keep that command if we are not gentle by nature? Gentleness is a fruit of the Spirit. We can't produce it on our own. It's something that God, by His Spirit, yields in us. God can bring a gentle spirit to a seriously strident soul.

That's true of my friend who didn't have a gentle bone in her body. As we were talking, a church deacon passed by and heard the comment. He had served as treasurer for more than thirty years and he knew the woman well. He paused and looked at her. "I've known you for a long time. You're not as harsh as you used to be. You've changed."

Could you use gentleness? I suppose we could try multiple tattoos to harness the harshness. Or we could ask the Holy Spirit to produce gentleness inside of us. I'll skip the tattoos and stick with the Spirit.

In your preaching, let your gentleness be evident to all. Gentleness isn't for wimps.

41

42 Preach about money

HWR

One of the topics that Christians need to hear and that preachers need to preach is the subject of money. Occasionally, you will hear a pastor apologize as he begins to preach on money. The church is in the midst of some kind of campaign and he says, "This is not my favorite topic, but I think we need to face the fact that Christians need to do something with their money."

We need to realize that the best time to preach on money is when you *don't* have to preach on money, when you are not trying to raise funds. If you read through the Gospels, when Jesus contrasts being a follower of His with not being a follower of His, the contrast is between a disciple of God and a disciple of money. You cannot serve God and money. If you decide to serve God, then you use your money to enhance His kingdom. If you decide to serve money, you'll use God like a hot water bottle on a cold winter's night.

We are not faithful to our people if we don't talk honestly, frankly, and biblically about the subject of money. We ought not be preaching on money simply because the church needs a new roof. We ought to be preaching on it regularly because the people in the church need a new heart for God. Today, in a materialistic society in which everywhere people turn they are being talked to about money, we just can't be silent about it.

I would urge you to think through what you believe about

money and, more than that, what God says about money. Take a day and look at the passages in the Gospels and in the Epistles in order to see what the Bible says about money. According to the Bible, money is not God's way of raising funds. It is His way of raising friends, of making friends for eternity. Frankly, if you've got money and you don't invest it in Christ's kingdom, then you are not really faithful as a follower of Christ.

42

I urge you, for the sake of Christ's kingdom, for the sake of your people, for your own sake, preach about money. Preach about it in the context of the Scriptures. Preaching about it is a responsibility that any follower of Christ has. Preach about it. When you preach about giving, you'd better be sure you are giving yourself. Preach about money.

43 We need reminders

JDA

In *The Silver Chair* by C. S. Lewis, Aslan gives Jill this command, "Seek the lost prince until either you have found him and brought him to his father's house, or else die in the attempt."

Jill says, "How, please? How am I going to do this?"

Aslan gives Jill four signs. They are a mixture of clear specifics and vague generalities, but they are sufficient for her to carry out her quest. Then Aslan sends her on her way with this exhortation, "Remember, remember the signs. Say them to yourself when you wake in the morning, and when you lie down at night, and when you wake in the middle of the night. And whatever strange things may happen to you, let nothing turn your mind from following the signs. I give you a warning, Jill. Here on the mountain I've spoken to you clearly. I will not often do so down in Narnia. On the mountain the air is clear and your mind is clear. As you drop down into Narnia, the air will thicken. Take great care that it does not confuse your mind. Remember the signs. Believe the signs. Nothing else matters."

Why do I recount this episode from *The Silver Chair*? To remind you that people need reminders. Repeatedly set before your people the cornerstones of our faith. Tell them over and over: "God loves you." "He has redeemed you." "We are a family." "Your name is written on His hands." "He carries you like a lamb, close to His heart." "A day of judgment is coming." To be sure, most of your listeners have heard these ideas before, but a reminder is like a beautiful sunrise that lights our way. Part of your job as a soul-watcher is to remind believers of the core truths of the faith that will help them make their way through this foggy world.

43

So don't be afraid to tell the old, old story, because people need reminders.

44 Good preachers own wastebaskets and use them

MDK

The longtime pastor Warren Wiersbe once said, "Good preachers own wastebaskets and use them." It's a funny image connecting your sermon to a garbage can.

You think about all of the hard work that you've poured into the sermon. Why would a wastebasket fit into all of this? Well, most of the time, we can't fit everything that we have prepared into a sermon. You're spending ten hours, perhaps twelve hours, fifteen hours, some of us even twenty hours exegeting the Scriptures. We're exploring what God has to say to the people of God back then and today. We do word studies. We do sentence diagramming. We translate the text. We find nuggets of wisdom from God's Word every single week. It's hard for us to pare it all down.

I worked with a youth pastor whom I loved dearly. He was an extrovert. What I noticed about him was that he wanted to fit everything he could into a single sermon. One of the dangers that we can fall into is that we want to fit everything we have gleaned from the Word of God into the sermon, that is, every good illustration, every good word study, all of the commentators' insights. "How can I fit all of this into the sermon?"

When we write sermons like that they can become lackluster, because they don't have a clear purpose. Sermons that are most effective have precision. They have a clear target.

When we allow all the things that we've studied to enter the sermon—yes, they might be good material; yes, they might be enriching; yes, they might be edifying—but for that particular sermon *all* of our exegetical morsels may not be what listeners need to hear on that day.

44

Sermon writing is about writing. I once heard that good writing is the art of good editing. How much time do we spend crafting our manuscript? When we write out a full manuscript, we're able to see the flow of the sermon. We literally see how we're getting from point to point. We see the relationship between sub-points. We see which illustrations need to be included and the word studies that need to be included. As we write out the manuscript, we're able to see what might be extraneous, what might need to be inserted, and determine even the stellar elements that are best left for another message.

You can't fit everything you learn into a thirty-minute sermon. You may have twenty-five minutes to forty-five minutes or somewhere in-between to preach. What is it that God wants us to convey to our listeners? What is *the* central truth that God wants us to communicate? What is that moving illustration that we need to include? What is that inspiring action from your parishioner's life that could really encourage the body of Christ? What is that morsel of truth that biblical writers understood that needs to be included in the sermon for that week? If it's not crucial to that sermon, we can leave it out. That's one of the beautiful elements of preaching week to week. There's always next Sunday, Lord willing, as long as we're alive. So there's no pressure to put in everything that we found in our study into a particular sermon. Warren Wiersbe is right: "Good preachers own wastebaskets and use them."

45 You need ten "'atta boys" for every one "you jerk"

HWR

I don't know a whole lot about running a seminary (I have been president of two of them), but one thing I have learned is that as a leader you have to find people doing something right more often than you catch people doing something wrong. In fact, if you don't commend people for what they are doing, it is hard to criticize them without their feeling resentful.

I don't know a whole lot about raising children (we have two, a son and a daughter, and neither of them is in prison last I checked), but we have discovered something about raising kids. You've gotta give them ten "'atta boys" for every one "you jerk." You've got to tell them what they are doing right more often than you tell them what they are doing wrong. I am convinced that if you don't keep that formula clear, give them ten "'atta boys" for every one "you jerk," you will be on their back rather than on their team.

I think that's true of preaching. Our tendency as preachers is to show people their failures, where they have come short, but that really isn't the biblical pattern. If you read the letters of Paul (e.g., the first letter he wrote to the Thessalonians) he says a great deal to them about what they are doing right, how much they meant to them, and how their example is an example for all the other churches in the first century.

I think we need to do that when it comes to preaching

the Scriptures. When we look at a virtue, it is important to illustrate it positively and not negatively (i.e., to show people somebody *doing* this—being patient, being kind, being courageous—rather than showing people folks who are unkind or cowards). I think it would be a practice sometime to stop and say, "Who in my congregation is doing this well?" Then point that person out to the people as you preach. It would be good to ask their permission to do it.

45

But I think we often discourage people. We set a bar in the Scriptures and talk to them about God's enabling power. Then they come back a week later and we've raised the bar. After a while, they get discouraged. But surely God is doing a work in the middle of your people. He is doing it in their lives. He is doing it as they work together.

So a wise leader, a good pastor, tells people what they are doing right more often than what they are doing wrong. Maybe the formula for raising children is a formula for developing Christians in church. Give them ten "'atta boys" for every one "you jerk." Why not try that the next time you have to preach? Show people those that they know who are doing it right rather than showing them people who are doing it wrong.

46 Go to the balcony

PMB

In his book *Getting to Yes*, the author and mediator William Ury talks about "going to the balcony." Ury describes the balcony as "a metaphor for a place of perspective, where we can keep our eyes on the prize." I think preachers need to get out of the pulpit every so often and climb up to the balcony.

Picture the balcony at your church building. I climbed a spiral, wooden staircase to get to ours. Sound equipment, a vacation Bible school banner, and a shepherd's crook from the pageant littered the creaky floorboards. Once my eyes were off the clutter, I scanned the sanctuary below. I got a bird's-eye perspective. Squirmy kids, still seniors, white hair, gray hair, blonde hair, one red-head, brown hair in braids and pony tails, the bald and balding.

The cross was the focal point of the sanctuary. It clung to a velvety red curtain, over the baptistery.

The pulpit was positioned beneath the cross, in front of the baptistery.

Yes, it was true that paint was peeling, the curtain was dusty, and more than a few light bulbs needed to be changed. But from the balcony, I saw the larger picture: the people, the cross, and the pulpit.

Sometimes we need a balcony perspective. It's easy to get caught up in programs and agendas and the nitty-gritty of pastoral ministry. But the bigger perspective reminds us that we are to preach the gospel of Jesus Christ to people who desperately need to hear it.

Preacher, do you need a new perspective? Climb on up to the balcony. You'll be reminded of your crucial task to preach the gospel of Jesus Christ to people who desperately need to hear it. Go to the balcony.

46

47 Praise your listeners before correcting them

MDK

There is a temptation in every preacher to begin and end every sermon with correction. Didn't Paul tell us in 2 Timothy 3:16 that "all Scripture is God-breathed and is useful for teaching, rebuking, correcting, and training in righteousness, so that the servant of God may be thoroughly equipped for every good work"? Yes, he did say that. So we follow suit and begin and end every sermon with correction, rebuke, and training in righteousness because it's good for our listeners. Their apathy needs to be shaken up a bit with some scolding, we say to ourselves.

While our responsibility as preachers is to teach, rebuke, correct, and train in righteousness, to equip the saints for good works, I'm not convinced that every sermon needs to start out with such stern exhortation. Perhaps we could be more gentle as we begin our sermons and praise our listeners before we correct them. As I read the book of Revelation, in particular Jesus' messages for the seven churches in Asia, He isn't always so quick to rebuke and correct as we are prone to do. In fact, Jesus often begins with praise and then moves to correction.

Here are a few examples. Jesus says to the church in Ephesus: "I know your deeds, your hard work and your perseverance. I know that you cannot tolerate wicked men, that you test those who claim to be apostles but are not, and have found them false. You have persevered and have endured hardships for my name, and have not grown weary. Yet I hold this against you: You have forsaken your first love. Remember the height from which you have fallen! Repent and do the things you did at first." Praise and then correct.

To the church in Pergamum, Jesus makes this observation: "I know where you live—where Satan has his throne. Yet you remain true to my name. You did not renounce your faith in me, even in the days of Antipas, my faithful witness, who was put to death in your city—where Satan lives. Nevertheless, I have a few things against you." Praise first and then rebuke.

To the church in Thyatira Jesus says: "I know your deeds, your love and faith, your service and perseverance, and that you are now doing more than you did at first. Nevertheless, I have this against you: You tolerate that woman Jezebel, who calls herself a prophetess." Praise first and then correct in righteousness.

While Jesus doesn't always follow this pattern, there is something to be said about offering praise to our listeners before correcting them. It's an attitudinal shift that we desire. I remember when the honeymoon phase at my church began to fade. We were now in the thick of ministry. I witnessed a lack of hunger and desire in my church for God and the apathy that exuded week after week. Without even knowing it, my sermons had become weekly bombs where I sent off missiles to the church by scolding and rebuking and correcting them in every sermon often from start to finish. It was only when someone pulled me aside one Sunday and asked me if I was alright. "Yes, I'm alright," I said. "Then why do you sound so angry at us?" Ah, I learned a great lesson that day. As a general disposition, people need to know that they are loved before they want instructions on how they ought to change. We can praise our listeners first for the ways they are being faithful to God before we rebuke and correct and train in righteousness. So give it a try, praise your listeners before correcting them.

47

Give your listeners verse numbers

48

MDK

How often have we heard preachers actually give their listeners verse numbers? What do I mean? When preaching a narrative passage or even an epistle, we may address the text generally. We may explain what the author is talking about. We may tell the story with wonderful images to create word pictures in their minds. But we can develop a habit of preaching where we forget to encourage people to look at their Bibles. So refer to the text. What is the text saying? Call out verse numbers. Get people into the Bible. Call people to read the Word as you are preaching it. We want to be able to have people look at the Word.

In this age of technology, we're faced with the challenge of congregants not bringing their Bibles to worship. We've settled for the fact that on our phone or iPad, we can access Scripture. We can pull up a Bible text at any time and look at particular passages that we're studying in the sermon. But one of the ways we can really benefit our listeners is to advocate bringing their Bibles to church and literally open them up to a particular passage. Help them see and read God's Word for themselves. Read it. Meditate on it. And see God's Word in print on a piece of paper.

One of the ways we can do this is to simply say, "Look with me at verse 4." Or, "Look with me at verse 32." This pro-

48

motes reverence for the Word of God. There is a sense of awe and reverence that we approach Scriptures with. This is God's Word. It's not just a story. It's God's love letter to His people. He's encouraging us to meditate on it just like the psalmist says in Psalm 119. The people of God are to meditate. They're supposed to have their minds dwell on God's Word—the richness and fullness of His Word. This Word gives life to the people. It guides our lives. It's a lamp for our feet and a light for our path. We feel reverence for God's Word when we hold the bounded cover of Scripture in our hands.

Biblical illiteracy is the norm today but we can assist our listeners in becoming increasingly biblically literate. How many times have we called out a book of the Bible to see our people fumble around looking for the text? Perhaps they have no idea how to locate prophetical books like Joel or Habakkuk or even one of the four Gospels. People just don't know how to navigate their way around Scripture. Give people a glimpse, by getting them to look at the text, and say, "How does this text, how does this particular verse, impact me?" If we look at narrative texts, instead of just telling the story, get them to look at verse 5. What does Jesus mean when he talks about the kingdom of God looking like a mustard seed? Get them to look at the verse and say, "Read this. Meditate on it. Think through what God wants to communicate to you in this particular verse." So one of the ways that we can equip our listeners to develop a passion, devotion, and love for God's Word is to simply give our listeners verse numbers.

Pastors are soul-watchers

49

JDA

Hebrews 13:17 says, "Obey your leaders and submit to them, because they are keeping watch over your souls as those will have to give an account." Pastors are soul-watchers. The Greek verb "to keep watch" means "to stay awake" or "to be on the alert." Pastors are to show diligent oversight for the spiritual well-being of their flock. The context of the book of Hebrews helps us understand. The Jewish-Christians were in danger of departing from the gospel. They were tempted to revert to the old ways of sacrifices, laws, and priesthood. So the author of Hebrews tells local church leaders to help believers keep believing the message about Christ and the new covenant. Local church leaders are charged with helping people not fall away by letting the gospel slip.

Pastors are soul-watchers. As when someone "watches" TV, teaching-pastors *observe* souls. We also *tend* souls as when the boy scout "watches" the fire. We keep the fire burning. We also *guard* souls as when the soldier stands "watch" through the night. Pastors are on sentry duty, protecting souls. Do you see yourself that way when you preach? Do you see yourself protecting souls, battling the world, the flesh, and the devil? Do you see yourself as contemplating and tending souls? This is our weighty calling.

One implication of pastoring as soul-watching is that

preaching and leadership belong together. Hebrews 13:17 is actually addressed to parishioners, not pastors. It says that they are to "obey their leaders and submit to them." So by implication, we see that preachers have authority. People are to submit to their spiritual leaders. True, submission does not sit well with American sensibilities. Nevertheless, the verse stands: "Obey your leaders and submit to them because they are keeping watch over your souls."

Another implication is that pastors will be held accountable. It is required of a steward that he or she be found faithful. A reward awaits those who shepherd well.

Listen again to the verse: "Obey your leaders and submit to them because they are keeping watch over your souls as those who will have to give an account." Pastors are soul-watchers.

Preachers can create a culture

MDK

Do you know that your church possesses a unique culture? Our churches have a culture. As preachers, we want to get to know the culture of our churches.

In his insightful book *Culture Making: Recovering Our Creative Calling,* Andy Crouch says that culture is not something only observed, but it is actually created. Culture is made by the people in our society, in our organizations, and even in our churches. Culture is all around us, but what cultures dominate in our church? Have you ever thought about that? What I'm talking about is not necessarily musical taste or political views or even the racial composition of our people but also the values, interests, pursuits, and dreams that they have—not just for themselves but for the kingdom of God.

I pastored a church in Colorado where the people were constantly tardy for worship. The worship service began at noon but people would trickle in at 12:05, 12:10, sometimes 12:15, and even 12:25. This was a recurring issue in our church. It was a culture—the culture of lateness. The problem came to the fore when one day visitors came into the sanctuary. The clock struck 12:06. As I looked at the clock, the visitors asked, "Doesn't your church service start at 12?" Embarrassingly, I said, "Yes, it does. I don't know where the people are."

I decided not to take that opportunity to correct the church publicly. But as I prayed about what types of cultures existed in our congregation, I noticed that there was this pervasive attitude of lateness in many of our people. I decided to broach the subject by preaching on it. Specifically, I preached a sermon about giving God our best in worship. I shared a hypothetical illustration about meeting the president of the United States and what type of attitude we would have when meeting him. Would we show up late? No. In fact, we would get there early. We would rehearse what we might say to him. We would prepare ourselves for that meeting.

50

In a similar way, I encouraged my listeners to consider how they approached Sunday worship in particular. Do we come with a sense of reverence? Do we come with a sense of giving God worth, which is what "worship" means? Are we giving God our best in worship? I used that preaching moment to address the culture of tardiness.

Another way to create culture in our ministry is to pattern it. Put your words into practice. I remember one time cleaning up the church foyer area where some children had made a mess by leaving crumbs all over the floor. As I cleaned up the mess, a church member came up to me and asked, "Why are you cleaning the church? You're the senior pastor. Why are *you* cleaning the church?" This was crying out for a teaching moment. I replied, "I am cleaning the church precisely because I am the senior pastor."

We create a culture by the way we preach, but we also create a culture by patterning what we're trying to communicate. Cleaning the church grounds was not technically in my job description. But it was something that I wanted to model for my church. Pastors are not exempt from service. We are servants first before anything else.

Lastly, we can create culture by praying. We want to be people who pray. We want to pray for the various cultures in our congregation to honor God, value God, and bring glory to God. We want to create a culture of generosity, of love, of service, of worship, of giving God glory, of bringing people to Christ, and of helping them become mature disciples. So what I want to encourage us to do is this: Create a church culture that will glorify God.

50

51   Strengthen yourself in the Lord

JDA

Being a pastor is hard. The flock expects you to be faster than a speeding bullet, stronger than a locomotive, and able to leap tall buildings with a single bound, but none of us is omnicompetent. Criticism comes when we don't meet people's expectations, but remember this: Strengthen yourself in the Lord. Take encouragement and hope by reminding yourself of the promises of God.

I find that idea in the story of David in 1 Samuel 30. While David was running from Saul, he gathered hundreds of malcontents and formed a guerrilla army. While they were protecting the borders of Israel, the Amalekites came to Ziklag, their home station, burned it with fire, and carried off their wives and children. When David and the men returned, the Bible says that they wept until they could weep no more. Just when things could not get any worse, David's own men turned against him, threatening to stone him. At that low point we read in 1 Samuel 30:6, "David strengthened himself in the LORD." When your pastorate is hard, strengthen yourself in the Lord.

How? Recall the promises of God. Recite, recall, rehearse, recount, and repeat the promises of God—the gates of hell will not prevail against His church. Though the mountains quake, He says to us, "I am the Lord." Though the seas rage and the mountains melt like wax, He is the same yesterday, today, and forever. Though this earthly tent is dismantled we have a heavenly one that will not fade. If we are faithless, He remains faithful. A crown is laid up for those who love His appearing. He has promised to never leave us or forsake us.

So when your pastorate is hard, strengthen yourself in the Lord.

51

52 The disease of modern preaching is its search after popularity

SMG

Charles Gore, formerly bishop of Worcester, Birmingham, and finally Oxford, wrote more than a century ago, "The disease of modern preaching is its search after popularity."

There is a certain disease that seems to bite, infect, and overtake us in ministry. We like to be liked. We like to be looked at. We like to be adored. It's a problem if we get ourselves ahead of Christ. I think Bishop Gore was right in saying that the disease of modern preaching is its search after popularity. In a consumeristic culture we're faced with a lot of people after star-power. Star preachers appear on television, on the Internet, at conferences, and in the publication world through books, tours, speaking circuits, magazine features, and polls. These preachers are raised to pedestals and platforms, adored and almost worshiped in a twenty-first-century marketed way. We live in a culture of self-importance. We're aware of these challenges that we face as preachers.

What often happens is that we believe our own press. Someone might approach us at the end of the service and tell us how wonderful we are, what a tremendous sermon we just preached, and right there the germ of popularity starts to take root in our souls.

The cult of personality has been emphasized in our twenty-first century. The tendency of people to be attracted to star-power is not new to the human race. Throughout the ages, men and women have been hailed by their contemporaries and adulated by them. Even the Bible charts the cry of Israel for a king and they got one, even though their king took attention away from God, the ultimate king. Saul, the first king, was compared in the popular culture of the day to the up-and-coming, eventual candidate for king—David. Following David's defeat of the threatening Philistine, Goliath, the heart of the crowd went toward the young, handsome victor: "Saul has slain his thousands," the people chanted, "and David his tens of thousands." The cult of personality is begun.

The popularity factor has become part of what it means to be a preacher in popular culture. No doubt, there has been a Luther, a Calvin, a Whitefield, a Wesley, an Edwards, a Spurgeon, and thousands of others. In his 1893 lectures on preaching, Robert F. Horton laments, "And before I go any further, let me utter my protest against the danger of popularity. *Popular preacher*—it is a term that fills one with misgiving. What has a preacher to do with popularity? Is it not enough that the disciple should be as his Lord?"

Horton gives us a great question to consider. It pushes us to think about our motives. Why do we preach? Why do we serve? Why do we do what we do? I trust it is not for popularity because that in and of itself is like a mist and it will evaporate before we know it. That is what happened to Saul. He thought he had the world by the tail, but it didn't happen. The same has happened to all kinds of preachers in these centuries. They have arisen in their popularity and they have been pulled down by their own deceit. Our call is to be not greater than our master but to follow our master. Our call is to recognize that we are utterly and totally dependent on Him because He is the one who receives all glory, praise, and honor, not ourselves.

These words by Bishop Gore are chilling words, but they are a good reminder to us. We, as preachers of God's Word, aren't to get ahead of God. Our task is to announce who God is to this generation. The disease of modern preaching is its search after popularity.

52

Guest preaching doesn't have to be a guessing game

MDK

Occasionally, or even regularly, we may be asked to preach somewhere other than our home church. That's called guest preaching. It's an honor to preach the Word on every occasion, but it's humbling when we're invited to deliver God's Word to another congregation. Guest preaching is not something that we want to take for granted or take lightly.

I want to remind us that guest preaching is not a guessing game. For those of us who've been pastors long enough, we know that at times it is difficult to preach even to our own congregations. While we are readily familiar with our people's struggles, there are still basic elements to their lives that are concealed from us. How much more obscure is the knowledge that we have about the congregations where we are supplying pulpits. Oftentimes we have very little information about the people in these congregations. So what are some things that we can keep in mind?

One of the best ways to get some insight into the lives of other church members is to send out a brief questionnaire to the pastor or elder of that congregation prior to beginning your sermon preparation. My colleague, Dr. Jeff Arthurs, gave me this tip as he shared with me how he sends to every church where he does pulpit supply a questionnaire that will help him more effectively prepare a message for unfamiliar people.

First, we can ask about the spiritual maturity level of the congregation. In his book, *Preaching with a Plan*, another colleague, Dr. Scott Gibson, helps us consider the spiritual maturity level of our people. Get a feel for the congregation in terms of their level of scriptural knowledge. Generally speaking, are they biblically literate? Are they obedient to the Word? Are they committed to loving and serving the church and wider community?

Second, we can find out about the generational variances in the church? Whom are you speaking to—mostly college students, young professionals, Baby Boomers, the elderly, a blend of each of these groups? What are their ages?

Third, find out about their vocations; that is, are they mostly professionals or blue-collar workers, are they educated or less educated? This information will guide our sermon preparation.

Fourth, what is the ethnic diversity in the church? Are there people from other ethnic and cultural backgrounds in the congregation that we will want to consider, or is the congregation fairly homogeneous? Get to know the variety of listeners you will be speaking to prior to the worship service.

Another set of questions to keep us from guessing is to ask about questions related to etiquette. What time should we arrive? What should we wear? How long should the sermon be? Are there any other responsibilities in the worship service that we should be prepared for? How many worship services do they offer on a Sunday? Recently, I failed to ask the church where I served as guest preacher what time they wanted me to arrive nor did they tell me. So I got to the church twenty minutes before the start of the service. As I found the reserved parking spot for me, which was in the middle of Boston, I noticed that I had to park very closely to another vehicle and barely fit into the spot. When I got out of my car, the head usher came over and looked at his watch, giving me a stern look, and said, "That's what happens when you're late!" I didn't realize that I was supposed to get there about thirty minutes prior to the time of worship. It was rather embarrassing to say the least.

Guest preaching is indeed an honor and we want to be well prepared for the moment. And it may help us to ask some basic questions before we stand up to preach. If we're able, send out a questionnaire, call up the pastor or worship leader, and make sure that we're prepared to preach for another church because guest preaching is not a guessing game.

53

54 Pastors are preachers and preachers are pastors

SMG

Pastors are preachers and preachers are pastors. If you think about it, as preachers, we have a responsibility to give men, women, boys, and girls the Word of God. We communicate to them the truth of the gospel, the truth of the Bible, Sunday in and Sunday out.

Sometimes as preachers we see ourselves as preachers only, that is, our role is only that of a preacher. I remember at my first church greeting worshipers at the door following the service. One particular member of my congregation, every Sunday, would shake my hand and say, "Good morning, preacher!" His occupation was a carpet-layer. I always wanted to say, "Good morning, carpet-layer!" because I did not necessarily see myself as only in the role as a preacher. I did that every Sunday. I prepared messages and worked toward that end, but my position as a preacher was not my only role. I did not want to be defined only as a preacher.

The work of a preacher is important work. We see that throughout the Scripture, from Genesis to Revelation, God uses preachers to communicate His Word. Most of us, I'm sure, are very comfortable with the role of being a preacher. But it is not our only role, is it? As preachers it is not that we just simply stand up and preach and then, from Sunday to Sunday (i.e., the days between Sundays), we are squirreled away doing nothing. Even our work as preachers has pastoral ends.

We are shepherds as the Bible calls us: "Be shepherds of God's flock" (1 Peter 5:2). Shepherds are pastors. We have a pastoral type of ministry. We care for our sheep. So in reality, not only are we preachers, but we are also pastors. It is through our preaching that we shepherd men and women. But it is not just through our preaching only that we shepherd. We shepherd through our leading of our congregation in Bible studies. We shepherd through visiting our congregation in their homes. We shepherd through prayer. We shepherd through relationships. We are pastors as well.

So this dual role—the role of a preacher and pastor—go hand in hand. We don't just preach—we love and we lead as pastors. That shows up in our preaching, in the way we preach, in the words we use as we preach, and in the attitude that we take toward our listeners as we preach. Is it not a great privilege to be not only a preacher but also a pastor?

Yes, pastors are preachers and preachers are pastors. This is a privileged role that we all share as we love our congregations, as we lead them. If you exclude the one (i.e., pastor) from the other (i.e., preacher), you can still be a good pastor. But, as a good pastor, your listeners will be much more willing to hear you. But, if you are not one who pastors and shepherds and loves your listeners, it is likely your listeners will find it difficult to hear you preach, or even follow you. These two roles, pastoring and preaching, are important roles—good twins—as we do the work of the Lord, as we live out our calling. Don't forget: Pastors are preachers and preachers are pastors.

54

55 A crown awaits elders who lead well

JDA

A crown awaits elders who lead well. That encouragement comes straight from God's Holy Word in 1 Peter 5:1–4: "So I exhort the elders among you as a fellow elder. . . . Exercise oversight, not under compulsion, but willingly, as God would have you; not for shameful gain, but eagerly; not domineering over those in your charge, but being examples to the flock. And when the chief Shepherd appears, *you will receive the unfading crown of glory.*"

I remind you of the promise of God: Elders who lead well have a crown awaiting them. Furthermore, I want you to know that I admire you as shepherds of the flock. The work of a pastor is harder than my work as a seminary professor. As a former pastor, and as a current elder, I have been on both sides of the fence, and I hold you in high esteem.

But my admiration is small potatoes compared to the promise of God, so I say to you on His behalf, "God values your work. He will give you a crown for voluntarily doing the work of an overseer, not under compulsion, not for gain, but by being a good example." The fact that He promises a crown reveals His heart, doesn't it? He values your work. So will you remember His promise? Remember it when the sheep bite. Remember it when you are in the tenth hour of exegeting the text and still can't crack the nut. Remember it when you're in your third evening meeting of the week after having worked all day as well. Remember that a crown awaits shepherds who lead well.

Thank you, shepherds, examples, pastors of the flock. I admire you, and God values your work, and He will demonstrate His appreciation when He gives the crown to those who lead well. Yes, a crown awaits elders who lead well.

55